URSTADT BIDDLE PROPERTIES

Urstadt Biddle Properties

The History of a REIT
1969-2012

Gene Brown

Copyright © 2008 by Urstadt Biddle Properties Inc.

Library of Congress Control Number:		2008905317
ISBN:	Hardcover	978-1-4363-5094-5
	Softcover	978-1-4363-5093-8
	Ebook	978-1-4691-0789-9

All rights reserved. No part of this book may be reproduced or transmitted in any form or by any means, electronic or mechanical, including photocopying, recording, or by any information storage and retrieval system, without permission in writing from the copyright owner.

This book was printed in the United States of America.

To order additional copies of this book, contact:
Xlibris Corporation
1-888-795-4274
www.Xlibris.com
Orders@Xlibris.com
49721

CONTENTS

Chapter One	REITs	7
Chapter Two	Hubbard Real Estate Investments	17
Chapter Three	Years Of Transition: The 1980s	43
Chapter Four	A New Business Plan	62
Chapter Five	Urstadt Biddle Properties	89
Chapter Six	A New Century	98
Chapter Seven	Successfully Negotiating Tough Times	126
Appendix I		143
Appendix II		147
Index		149

Chapter One

REITS

REITS Evolve Into Entrepreneurs
—*Retail Traffic*, March 2004

We've come a long way since a new sector of the real estate industry came quietly into being in 1960. Attracting little public attention at its birth, the business in which Urstadt Biddle Properties today thrives did not even have any active firms until almost a year after the passage of the 1960 federal legislation that made real estate investment trusts (REITs) possible. In fact, it would take almost a decade before these trusts began to make a real impact on real estate investment.

To anyone familiar only with today's REITs, those first real estate investment trusts would seem like alien entities. "Entrepreneurship" was hardly on the minds of those who in 1960 came up with the idea for this new form of passive, bondlike investment. In fact, its architects, who envisioned something we might call hands-off management-lite for the first REITs, would themselves hardly recognize today's involved management practiced by Urstadt Biddle Properties.

The Beginning

Somebody once said that what this country needs is a good five-cent cigar. Inflation has long since put that cheap pleasure hopelessly out of reach. But that traditional capstone to a hearty and satisfying dinner did figure in the creation of another, much different need that Congress fulfilled in 1960. That year, it tacked onto the Cigar Excise Tax Extension, an amendment to the Internal Revenue Code of 1954. The amendment was known as the Real Estate Investment Trust Act.

The demand for the creation and growth of real estate investment trusts—or as they quickly became known by their abbreviation, REITs—was a product of post–World War II and Korean War prosperity. As his eight-year presidency drew to a close in 1960, President Eisenhower, who signed the REIT law on September 14 of that year, could boast that real wages had increased 20 percent under his watch, with family income up 15 percent. A growing middle class was acquiring homes in the suburbs and other amenities of the good life. An expanding economy was producing jobs with good incomes and generating, as well, diverse investment opportunities for the cash that was now available to many families beyond what they needed for life's basics. Much of that cash found its way into the stock market, particularly through mutual funds.

The Great Crash of 1929 temporarily had taken the steam out of the notion that stock ownership was a prudent idea for the average middle-class investor. But the Great Depression aversion to stocks had largely receded by 1950 when Merrill Lynch, Pierce, Fenner, & Smith could boast one hundred branch offices nationwide. In the 1950s, mutual funds had become a particularly popular form of investment in stocks for the average family. Rather than try to pick the "winners" among individual stocks, many people relied on these syndicates of professionally managed securities portfolios to build a nest egg for retirement or a child's college education. Mutual funds enabled millions of average Americans to put a modest amount of savings to work through the joint ownership of shares in American industry.

Mutual funds, as we know them, had been around since the Massachusetts Investor's Trust was organized in Boston in 1924 and taken public in 1928. In the early 1940s, the mutual fund industry had grown to eighty funds with assets of $500 million. But it was the general prosperity of the Eisenhower years, and particularly the encouraging performance of the stock market, which in 1954 finally surpassed the pre-Depression 1929 Dow Jones Average high of 381.17 and went on to hit 685 in 1960, that increased consumer interest in this convenient form of investment. By 1960, there were 160 mutual funds with upward of 2.5 million shareholders. Some of the funds, such as the Dreyfus Fund organized in 1951, had become almost household names. With $17 billion to invest as the 1960s began, the funds had become a significant factor in the American economy.

But none of this money was going into real estate. The physical infrastructure of the booming American economy, its single-family homes and apartment complexes, retail stores and shopping centers, hotels, warehouses, office buildings, and factories, not to mention the land on which they were built and the mortgages that financed them, did offer potential prime investment opportunities. But the nature of investment in real property limited participation either to developers, banks, insurance companies, and other institutions that financed construction, or affluent individuals who could afford the price of a limited partnership. Although real estate syndicates had been around since the 1880s, they were private, few in number, and did not spread ownership around sufficiently to make them affordable and practical for most people.

The only kind of real estate investment that touched most average Americans was the house they lived in. But unlike the present, in which the sometimes-rapid increase in value of residential real estate has encouraged consumers to regard their home as virtually a part of their investment portfolio, at least until the subprime bust of 2007, houses in the 1950s were still primarily places in which to live. This was even more the case in large cities where apartment condos and co-ops were still mostly a thing of the future. In 1960 in New York City, for example, you could rent an eight-room apartment with a view on fashionable Central Park West for $425 a month. But if ownership was on your mind, you would have to buy the building.

Further, even if one had the money, real estate, unlike stock ownership, was not a liquid investment. Investors could buy or sell stock with a call to their broker, but there was no such fluid and accessible market for real estate. Managing real estate investments demanded one's time and attention; ownership posed considerable risk and was hardly suited for the casual investor lacking specialized knowledge in the field. But in the prosperous times of the late 1950s, interest was building for widening access to real estate's potential for capital growth and healthy cash flow. And in 1960, the door was pushed open.

The Real Estate Investment Trust Act

Inspired by the success of mutual funds, REITs were initially designed to resemble as much as possible those pools of stocks. They were meant to be passive enterprises, merely conduits through which the average person could invest in real estate. The 1960 law specifically structured REITs so that they would pay dividends. At least 90 percent of a REIT's taxable income—later increased to 95 percent—had to be returned to shareholders as dividends. In return, the REIT paid no federal taxes on that revenue paid out as dividends. The dividends were only taxed when the recipients paid their individual income tax. A minimum of 75 percent of a REIT's gross income had to come from real property assets. REITs were also structured to prevent concentration of ownership in a few hands. The REIT needed a minimum of one hundred shareholders, and five or fewer shareholders could own no more than 49 percent of total shares outstanding.

REITs were not originally intended to be active real estate businesses themselves, actually managing and operating properties and buildings. A board of directors or trustees oversaw the REIT's operations; but their function—in the case of an equity REIT such as Urstadt Biddle Properties, one based on the ownership of real property instead of mortgages—was really to give final approval to the activities of an outside advisory body, the "advisor," which actually determined an appropriate investment program for the REIT's portfolio and initiated and negotiated the deals to acquire the property that filled it. This advisory body was the counterpart of a mutual fund's managers who, of course, do not actually manage and operate the businesses represented by the stocks in their fund's portfolio. In fact, virtually everything that a REIT did would have to be done through outside, independent contractors, from which the REIT could not derive any income.

One of the problems this mandated advisor would create involved an inherent conflict of interest. The company creating or sponsoring the real estate investment trust would also staff the advisor. The advisor would charge the real estate investment trust a fee for its services. This, in effect, would be the bulk of the managerial cost of running the trust. But it was in the sponsor's interest to have the advisor maximize those fees, whereas in an independently run real estate business, management would see it as their mission to minimize managerial costs, making the company more efficient and thus producing greater profitability for the company and value for shareholders.

The 1960 federal REIT law did not require that REIT assets be equity based. They could generate their cash flow by lending money secured by real property collateral; and in fact, the first REITs—including Bradley Real Estate Investors, Continental Mortgage Investors, First Mortgage Investors, First Union Real Estate, Pennsylvania REIT, and Washington REIT—were mortgage based. Since brokers and bankers sponsored these first real estate investment trusts, it's not surprising that they would opt for a form of operation most familiar to them.

Technically, people who bought REIT shares were buying a beneficial interest in a trust, not a "stock," in the ordinary sense of the word. But in practice, it was close to the same thing. There was a daily market for these shares; they could be purchased in relatively small quantities, unlike actual real property. Their value could be determined precisely at any given time—try doing that with an individually owned piece of property!—and they were as liquid as common stocks.

In its issue of July 1, 1961, *Forbes* heralded the future: "Just around the corner is a small but possibly potent new competitor for the investor's dollar. A mutual fund of a kind, the new company will invest not in stocks or bonds but in mortgages. Its name: First Mortgage Fund, a closed-end real estate investment trust. Its objective: to invest its funds in high-yielding first mortgages and, by distributing 90% of its net income, to avoid federal corporation taxes."

Off to a Slow Start

REITs did not exactly take the investment community by storm. They were new, and people were wary about investing in something for which there was no track record. Stockbrokers, from whom many investors got advice about what to buy, saw a "real estate" label on REIT shares; and real estate was still off the beaten path for Wall Street. On the other hand, those already oriented toward real estate as an investment saw REITs as just another kind of Wall Street stock. No more than about ten REITs of any substantial size would emerge during that first decade; and none, at first, involved significant amounts of capital.

Until the late 1960s, the industry moved at a snail's pace. A notable step forward occurred in June 1965 when Continental Mortgage Investors became the first REIT listed on the New York Stock Exchange. In 1968, Robert Lurie and Sam Zell founded Equity Group Investments, a private real estate firm from which they would later generate Equity Office Properties Trust, Equity Residential, and Equity Lifestyle Properties, and REIT Capital Trust, Inc., some of the industry's largest companies.

Despite being something of an investment backwater, the early REITs did fairly well; and by the end of the decade, Wall Street began taking REITs more seriously. The September 1970 launch of *Realty Trust Review*—later *Realty Stock Review*, the first periodical to cover the real estate industry exclusively—was one signal that real estate investment trusts were arriving. More important, the National Association of Real Estate Investment Trusts, or NAREIT, began its index of equity REITs in 1972.

REITs really arrived as the 1960s gave way to the 1970s. As Ralph L. Block put it in his *Investing in REITs: Real Estate Investment Trusts*: "Between 1968 and 1970, with the willing assistance of many investment bankers, the industry produced fifty-eight new mortgage REITS. Most of these used a modest amount of shareholders' equity and huge amounts of borrowed funds to provide short-term loans to the construction industry, which in turn, built hundreds of office buildings throughout the United States."

In fact, REITs played an unfortunate role in the overbuilding that occurred during this period. Real estate is a cyclical business; and REITs were early on subject to the same boom, overexpansion, recession, and period of opportunities-to-buy-good-properties-at-favorable-rates that started the next boom, as were other types of real estate investments. The inflation of the early 1970s (higher interest rates hit especially hard at mortgage REITs) and overbuilding produced a painful real estate recession, one of the worst ever, that began in 1973-74 and persisted into the later part of the decade. Between 1972 and 1975, the NAREIT index lost about 90 percent of its value. Mortgage REITs in 1972 had a market value of $774 million. Two years later the number of mortgage REITs had actually increased, from eighteen to twenty-two, but their total market value had dropped to $244 million. The *Wall Street Journal*'s headline on January 21, 1974, encapsulated the situation: "Realty Trust Woes." Ultimately there were significant failures among the mortgage REITs. Continental Mortgage Investors, the second largest REIT and the first listed on the NYSE, would default on its bank debt in December 1975, tainting the value of shares of all REITs. When the industry recovered, it would be equity REITs—such as Hubbard Real Estate Investments, now known as Urstadt Biddle Properties—that would dominate.

Even in the midst of hard times, the federal government began to modify the laws governing REITs, giving them more flexibility in their operations and allowing them to perform some of the functions of actual real estate companies. A 1974 law enabled REITs to directly manage for ninety days any property they acquired through foreclosure or default before turning it over to a management company. The Tax Reform Act of 1976 permitted REITs to be set up as corporations as well as trusts.

Prosperity returned to the real estate business in the early 1980s. But again, the surge of investment enthusiasm led to overbuilding. One element in this overexuberant market was the infusion of capital derived from the appeal of limited partnerships as tax shelters, a product of the Economic Recovery Act of 1981. This provision of the act created a motive for retaining property even when its return on invested capital might not reasonably justify such behavior, since it provided a "shelter" for profits created from other investments. REITs, given their structure, could not pass through tax losses. Limited partnerships not only diverted money that might have gone into REITs but also bid up the cost of borrowed capital and pushed the price of attractive properties higher and higher, since they did not have to worry as much as REITs did about how well such properties would perform.

REITs Become Self-Managing

The Tax Reform Act of 1986 undercut the value of limited partnerships and the tax shelters that they had offered investors. But more important for REITs, in the long run, this change in the tax laws recognized that REITs weren't exactly the same as stock mutual funds. With an investment base in real estate, the trusts needed to actively manage and operate the property they owned to maximize its value for shareholders. As was, and still is, the case with making a profit from real estate, passive investment was inefficient when it came to real property. Hands-on oversight and supervision were essential elements if significant profits were to be realized.

The 1986 act served as a kind of declaration of independence for REITs. It set them free to manage their own businesses internally. They no longer had to contract portfolio management out to an advisor. REIT management could now actually manage their properties, using skill and entrepreneurial spirit to grow their enterprise in the most efficient ways possible, like the real estate businesses they had finally become. REITs could now actively lease, retenant, and improve properties, creating more opportunities to achieve capital gains as well as to pay steady dividends.

New forms of REITs also appeared. While REITs were initially structured to resemble mutual funds, there were at first no REITs that existed simply to hold pools of shares of other REITs, as mutual funds did with stocks. That changed in January 1985, with the establishment of the National Real Estate Stock Fund, the first mutual fund for REITs. REIT investors could, for the first time, buy a package of real estate investment trusts. As the publication *Financial Planning* noted at the time, "the fund's main advantage is the flexibility to shift as real estate cycles change."

In the mid-1980s, REITs received a big publicity boost when the Rockefeller brothers, in a complicated transaction, created Rockefeller Center Properties, turning their twelve famous midtown buildings into a REIT. Rockefeller Center Properties financed the mortgage through the sale of several types of securities, including shares of common stock.

None of this, of course, did away with the real estate cycle. Investors might have had reason to be pleased with the steady flow of REIT dividends in the late 1980s. But had they looked more closely at the performance of many REITs, they would have been more concerned. Gauging REIT performance by the industry's standard measure of funds from operations, or FFO—net income plus depreciation less profit or loss from sale of property—many REITs were struggling. Inevitably, the price of REIT stocks reflected that struggle, and the late 1980s into the beginning of the 1990s was not a good time for REIT investors.

The stock market crash in the fall of 1987 didn't help. The downturn inevitably hit hard at office leasing and hurt consumers through declines in the value of their homes and apartments. In its issue of October 20, 1987, in the wake of the crash, *The New York Times* interviewed several people who had their fingers on the pulse of the local economy in the New York City metropolitan area. One of them was UBP's current chairman, Charles J. Urstadt, then chairman of the real estate firm of Pearce, Urstadt, Mayer, & Greer, Inc., Urstadt told the paper: "When the margin calls come, a lot of people are going to be looking at assets they can sell, and if real estate is one of them, they may be in for a shock."

Inevitably, bad times paved the way for something better. REIT share value recovered; and as now self-managing businesses, thanks to the Tax Reform Act of 1986, they were primed to participate in the financial boom that Americans would experience in the 1990s. Indeed, REITs in the 1990s finally began to take their place as what they had been intended to be from the first: major investment opportunities for the average person. An important factor in putting REITs in the company of other more familiar investments was the spate of major IPOs that occurred in the early 1990s.

In 1991, Kimco Realty Corporation went public with an IPO that made Wall Street and the investing public sit up and take notice. The Roslyn, New York-based firm, which then owned and operated 126 neighborhood shopping centers, raised $126 million with its offering, 40 percent of which was taken by institutional investors, yet another indication that REITs were becoming normalized as investments. The company earmarked the proceeds to pay down its substantial debt, approximately 50 percent of its asset value, compared to the industry average of 34 percent. "Kimco won't be administered by independent managers, relying instead on in-house people," the *Wall Street Journal* noted at the time, "and insiders hold almost 50% of the stock, among the highest ownership shares in the industry. That situation should erase any incentive for managers to milk the company for fees." The inefficiencies and potential conflict of interest inherent in the pre-1986 REITs with their "advisors" were obviously still on some minds.

Also in 1991, New Plan Realty Trust, an early REIT organized in 1972, became the first publicly traded REIT to achieve a $1 billion equity market capitalization. A year later, shopping mall mogul A. Alfred Taubman's Taubman Centers went public, motivated by Taubman's need to clear a substantial amount of the owner's personal debt. The REIT held nineteen enclosed shopping malls in eleven states, with over 21 million square feet of space.

Most impressively, REITs were raising capital during a recession when other sources of funds had all but dried up. The trusts were gaining recognition and respect in the field of real estate and among the investing public for their relative solidity. While others in the real estate sector were at best struggling and, at worst, not surviving, REITs were more than holding their own. "REITs are the real estate attack group," *National Real Estate Investor* quoted Louis J. Garday, who headed Burnham Pacific Properties, a San Diego REIT. "REITs emerged from the 1980s unscarred. We just kind of kept our head down and our earnings up. When everyone else in the industry was being slaughtered, we are still plugging along paying dividends, increasing our cash flow."

Stemming from this period was, finally, the increasingly widespread notion that REITs made good investments. Academic studies began to appear that confirmed what many in the industry had been noticing: as often as not, depending on the range of years being studied, REITs outperformed the S&P 500. While they generally followed the direction of the stock market, REITs were less volatile than stocks. A carefully chosen REIT or group of REITs therefore offered a good way to diversify a portfolio.

The public began to realize that by their nature, REITs usually do not see enormous increases in their earnings in any given year. And they certainly don't see them overnight. The upside of that was that investors did not have to worry about phantom price/earnings ratios with this investment. Nobody would confuse a REIT with a roller coaster.

Increases in REIT equity in 1993 from stock offerings exceeded the total amount of capital REITs had raised through this method in the previous thirteen years. By the mid-1990s, real estate "brand names" such as Kimco, Taubman Centers, and Simon Property Group, which had taken advantage of the favorable investment climate to "securitize" their holdings in the form of REITs, had put the industry on the map with brokers and investors. Simon Property's 1995 IPO was the largest to date.

The 1991 adoption by NAREIT of funds from operations, or FFO, as the standard by which REIT performance should be measured, was another sign that REITs were coming of age, although the Securities and Exchange Commission would not similarly recognize FFO until 2003.

The later part of the 1990s once again brought a downturn. Enthusiasm had gotten out of hand, some share prices had become unreasonably high, and too many new shares were coming on the market. Consequently, the price of REIT shares declined. But before long, the reduced price made them good values, and the cycle turned toward the positive side. That trend would continue through the middle of the new century's first decade.

In 1996, real estate titan Sam Zell launched a hostile takeover bid for Chateau Properties, a move that some in the investment press viewed as symbolic of the industry's maturity and acceptance as part of the normal investment scene. But it was not the first time such an acquisition of a REIT was attempted, despite claims to the contrary by journals such as the *Investment Dealer's Digest* (Oct 28, 1996), as will be seen shortly when we turn to the story of Urstadt Biddle Properties.

In 1993, the tax law had been modified to make it easier for pension plans to put their money into REITs. In 1996, in an IRS ruling, a residential REIT was allowed to include in its real estate operations the provision of cable TV service to tenants. The next year such services were codified in the law, and the government made it easier for foreigners to invest in US REITs. A further modification in the laws governing REITs came in 1999 when they were permitted to start and own subsidiaries. The REIT Improvement Act of 2004 made it even easier for foreign capital to flow into REITs and substituted possible financial penalties instead of loss of REIT tax status for unintentional violations of REIT regulations.

In October 2001, REITs finally made it into the S&P 500. The first REIT listed was Equity Office Properties Trust, followed a month later by Equity Residential. In January 2002, *Forbes* began an annual REIT rating list.

In the first years of the 2000s, REITs began to be important components of many 401(k) plans, a phenomenon heavily promoted by NAREIT; and foreign pension plans began substantial investments in US REITs. On the downside, many REITs complained that the Sarbanes-Oxley law of 2002, which imposed more rigid auditing requirements on companies as a result of a few widely publicized corporate scandals, was putting an unnecessary strain on their bottom line. Small cap REITs such as Urstadt Biddle Properties felt especially encumbered by these new requirements, but efforts to reform the law have as yet proven fruitless.

The success of the REIT as a means of investing in real estate spread rapidly beyond America's shores after 2000. The *International Herald Tribune* on December 20, 2003, pointed out that "a growing worldwide appetite for safe and stable returns has led to a rush around the world to establish real estate vehicles modeled on REIT's. In the past few years, REITs have been introduced in France, Japan, Singapore, South Korea and Hong Kong, while countries like Britain, long skeptical of such tax-transparent vehicles, are giving REIT's a fresh look." During 2003, the *Journal of Financial Planning* advised, REITs scored their greatest annual gain since 1976. In 2004, spurred on by low interest rates, more than twenty-five REITs went public, five times the number in the previous year. Equity REITs returned 12.16 percent in that year, according to NAREIT.

In 2005, *Investment Dealer's Digest* reported "that the real estate investment trust (REIT) structure is drawing a crowd. An increasing number of mortgage companies are changing their stripes to become REITs, and others in the mortgage origination business may be drawn to the vehicle as well."

In 2006, Standard & Poor's began to classify REITs as a separate industry. The addition of Kimco and Boston Properties to the Standard & Poor's 500 index in 2006 brought the total of REITs in the index to eleven and was expected to create about $1.7 billion of demand for these stocks by index funds.

The REIT industry today is almost twenty times as large as it was fifteen years ago. REITs own somewhere between 10 percent and 15 percent of all institutionally owned commercial real estate in America, worth approximately $400 billion. More than 150 REITs are traded on the New York Stock Exchange, with a market capitalization of more than $265 billion.

The REIT industry had grown tremendously since it was created in 1960. A form of investment once characterized as "exotic," when noticed at all, has entered the mainstream, its abbreviation now almost as familiar as the likes of "IPO." It's no longer unusual to see statements such as the one that *Barron's* made in its issue of November 10, 2005: "We believe REITs may be the best and most diversified way to publicly own commercial real estate for individual investors."

But this is the big picture. Nothing better illustrates the way an industry develops than following the story of one company in it. The story of the formation and early years of Hubbard Real Estate Investments (HREI), the transformation of HREI into HRE, and its evolution, in turn, into Urstadt Biddle Properties will show in microcosm some of the REIT characteristics and trends just discussed, as well as bring to the fore the unique spirit, ideas, and business strategy that have made Urstadt Biddle Properties one of the foremost success stories in its field.

Chapter Two

HUBBARD REAL ESTATE INVESTMENTS

The company that would evolve into Urstadt Biddle Properties had its origins in a decision made at Merrill Lynch, Pierce, Fenner & Smith in the late 1960s. Charles Merrill, founder of the brokerage firm, had pioneered bringing Wall Street to Main Street, promoting the idea that common stocks were an appropriate investment for the middle-income investor. As a brokerage firm, Merrill Lynch was, as well, a very significant player on the other side of the line between investor and investment, bringing IPOs to market and advising corporations in their dealings with the financial markets and with potential acquisitions and suitors.

The Merrill Lynch CEO in those years, Winthrop Lenz, a Princeton graduate who had come to the firm when it merged with E. A. Pierce in 1940, came up with the idea to sponsor a REIT based on a sale and leaseback mode of operation. Sale and leaseback was a (sometimes deceptively) "simple" financing technique. The REIT would buy a property, say a newly built warehouse or one under construction, from the company that owned it. The company that sold the property would simultaneously lease it back from the REIT. The company leasing the property gained the advantage of 100 percent financing of its new construction because all of the capital that would otherwise have been tied up in the structure it had just built came back to it from the sale and could then be used for other purposes—buying or building other warehouses, for example. The developer still had the use of the structure it had just built, but instead of owning the property, it now rented it from the REIT on a long-term lease.

In practice, the details of such a transaction could be a lot more complicated. For example, in October 1971, the Hubbard Real Estate Investment Trust Board of Trustees would consider a sale-leaseback arrangement involving a warehouse that the W. T. Grant Company was building in Albany, Georgia. According to the minutes of the board meeting, "the Trust would purchase the land for not in excess of $300,000 and lease it back to the builder, Unitco Realty and Construction Co., Inc., for 25 years at a net rental of approximately $26,100 (8.7% constant). The Trust would then loan the builder the cost of the building and improvements, the loan to be secured by a first mortgage on the building and on the leasehold interest, the loan to be repaid over 25 years at 7 1/2% interest on the outstanding balance (8.7% constant). W. T. Grant would execute a sub-lease as tenant of Unitco Realty and Construction Co., Inc. and this sub-lease would be assigned to the Trust as security for its loan. In addition, the Trust would have the option to determine the ground lease after the fifth year."

How did a REIT benefit from a sale-leaseback arrangement? It structured the lease on the property so that over the course of the lease, its original investment would be returned to it plus a fixed return on that investment. Typically that return might be 8-9 percent, with the lease running twenty to thirty years. Tenants could renew the lease, but at a lower, or "step-down" rent that amounted to about two-thirds of the original rent. Since the tenants, under a net lease, would be responsible for maintenance, insurance, taxes, and the like, the REIT's operating costs would be negligible. If this sounds more like something that one might expect when purchasing a bond rather than running a real estate operation, it's no accident. The whole transaction was very bondlike. The REIT's aim was to ensure a reliable flow of cash that would enable it to pay a just-as-reliable dividend to its shareholders. It hoped that the value of the asset would increase, but that was not a primary goal; and the REIT did not engage in activities that one would expect to find in a real estate business, such as renovating the premises or seeking new and better tenants, that would add value to and increase the revenue stream from the property.

As long as the tenant remained in business (didn't "default," continuing the bond analogy or, in this case, go bankrupt and break the lease) and as long as inflation did not get out of hand, the deal would provide the REIT with a steady, reliable cash flow year after year that would enable it to pay steady dividends and produce, through depreciation, which did not have to be distributed to shareholders a certain amount of excess capital that could be deployed in other investments. But the potential for growth, under the circumstances, would be minimal. Such investments were not so much managed as administered. Entrepreneurship, an important characteristic in most real estate businesses, was absent.

And what was in it for companies such as Merrill Lynch that sponsored this type of REIT that actually created this new investment entity? For one thing, although Merrill Lynch would not get a commission for selling stock in the REIT, it would benefit because the REIT's operations would neatly dovetail with the needs of some of Merrill Lynch's clients. The REIT would negotiate sale-leaseback deals with those clients, providing them with 100 percent financing for new stores, offices, or warehouses. Just as important, Merrill Lynch would also benefit from fees the REIT would pay it for investment advice and other services. The separate "advisor" required by the real estate investment trust law performed services for the REIT that independent real estate businesses would normally perform themselves.

The relationship between the REIT, its sponsor, and the advisory body had the potential for conflict of interest no matter how pure the intentions of the people involved. In form, the new REIT may have appeared to be independent; but in practice, it was closely tied to—really a part of—Merrill Lynch. While this setup never produced anything legally problematic in the course of this particular REIT's early years, it was far from ideal; and ultimately, it would need to be changed.

True, the REIT's board of trustees, with independent members unconnected to Merrill Lynch, acted as a watchdog for the shareholders' interests. But the trustees did not initiate acquisitions or formulate a business plan. Those were functions of the advisory body, which collected fees from the REIT but had loyalties divided between the Trust and Merrill Lynch, its parent company. Further, the trustees owned very little stock in the REIT, limiting their direct connection to and self-interest in the REIT's performance.

Setting Up Hubbard Real Estate Investments

To set the ball rolling, Merrill Lynch CEO Lenz wanted to first create a department within his firm specializing in sale-leaseback financing. Merrill Lynch had brokered real estate deals and sold stocks and bonds related to such transactions, but had no experience with directly running a real estate operation. So Lenz went outside his firm for someone to head the new department. He chose Morry Hubbard, an old friend, who with his brother John ran the corporate and real estate financing firm of Hubbard, Westervelt & Mottelay, which was experienced in handling sale leasebacks. But Morry Hubbard had other ideas about what sort of relationship he wanted to have with the big brokerage firm. He suggested that Merrill Lynch buy his company.

Eight months later, in October 1968, they had a deal. Merrill Lynch acquired the Hubbard firm, personnel from which would serve as the advisor to the new REIT sponsored by Merrill Lynch, to be called Hubbard Real Estate Investments. Merrill Lynch tapped as the new REIT's president Ralph G. Coburn, a lawyer and senior vice president and director of Hubbard, Westervelt & Mottelay. Coburn had served on the staff of Admiral Chester W. Nimitz, commander of the US fleet in the Pacific during World War II, eventually retiring with the rank of rear admiral.

Coburn went into his new job quite clear-eyed. He had no illusions about the independence of the new venture, nor would he make any analogies between his own position and commanding a warship. "They owned us," he would later acknowledge, referring to Merrill Lynch. The new company would "do what they said."

The Hubbards assembled a board of trustees that included Guardian Life Insurance CEO George T. Conklin, Jr. Besides serving on other boards, Conklin was also director of the National Bureau of Economic Research. Also serving on the board were John F. Meck, vice president of Dartmouth College, the Hubbards' alma mater; Joseph Taggart, dean emeritus of New York University's Graduate School of Business Administration; and Richard S. Willis, a real estate and mortgage consultant.

The Trust Begins

Hubbard Real Estate Investments was formally organized as a real estate investment trust in Boston on July 7, 1969. Massachusetts law made it advantageous to form the Trust and headquarter it in that state. At the board of trustees first meeting, Coburn was formally chosen president of the Trust and it was agreed that trustees would receive a per annum fee of $6,000, an amount typical at the time. Two weeks later the board approved Arthur Andersen LLP as HREI's auditor, and each trustee agreed to buy one hundred shares of the Trust. In hindsight, this was really a token figure, creating a situation in which a few men who had next to nothing at stake in the Trust would be ratifying decisions that would determine the Trust's future and fortunes—not to mention the return on HREI shareholder's investments.

One early task was to find office space in Boston. HREI located there, according to the minutes of a special meeting of the trustees on October 2, 1969, because "such a location seems desirable from the standpoint of state and local taxation and would relate the Trust's activities more significantly to Massachusetts, its state of organization."

Next came the job of raising capital to launch the company. Coburn found himself part of a "dog and pony" show, traveling around the country to Merrill Lynch branch offices, covering the particulars on the new venture and, hopefully, getting the "troops" fired up for the big sale. In November 1969, the Trust's IPO of 4 million shares, priced at $25 a share, went out. Within weeks, after Merrill Lynch and its syndicate of underwriters had done their job, there were twenty-five thousand HREI shareholders. By May 1970, just six months later, the company would be listed on the New York Stock Exchange.

This advertisement is not an offering. No offering is made except by a Prospectus filed with the Department of Law of the State of New York and the Bureau of Securities, Department of Law and Public Safety of the State of New Jersey. Neither the Attorney General of the State of New York nor the Bureau of Securities of the State of New Jersey has passed on or endorsed the merits of this offering.

NEW ISSUE   November 7, 1969

Hubbard Real Estate Investments

4,000,000 Shares of Beneficial Interest
(Without Par Value)

Price $25 Per Share

Copies of the Prospectus may be obtained in any State in which this announcement is circulated from only such of the undersigned or other dealers or brokers as may lawfully offer these securities in such State.

Merrill Lynch, Pierce, Fenner & Smith
Incorporated

Drexel Harriman Ripley Incorporated	Glore Forgan, Wm. R. Staats Inc.	Salomon Brothers & Hutzler
Stone & Webster Securities Corporation	Wertheim & Co. Crédit Lyonnais Corporation	Paribas Corporation
Bache & Co. Incorporated	Bear, Stearns & Co. Clark, Dodge & Co. Incorporated	Dominick & Dominick, Incorporated
Francis I. duPont, A. C. Allyn, Inc.	Equitable Securities, Morton & Co. Incorporated Goodbody & Co.	Hallgarten & Co.
W. E. Hutton & Co.	Ladenburg, Thalmann & Co. W. C. Langley & Co.	F. S. Moseley & Co.
Shearson, Hammill & Co. Incorporated	Shields & Company Incorporated G. H. Walker & Co. Incorporated	Wood, Struthers & Winthrop Inc.
Blair & Co., Inc.	Dick & Merle-Smith H. Hentz & Co. Hirsch & Co.	Johnston, Lemon & Co.
Spencer Trask & Co. Incorporated	Tucker, Anthony & R. L. Day Robert W. Baird & Co. Incorporated	Bateman Eichler, Hill Richards Incorporated
J. C. Bradford & Co., Incorporated	Dain, Kalman & Quail	The Robinson-Humphrey Company, Inc.
A. E. Ames & Co. Incorporated	Ball, Burge & Kraus Cogan, Berlind, Weill & Levitt, Inc.	Crowell, Weedon & Co.
Fahnestock & Co.	First of Michigan Corporation Fulton, Reid & Staples, Inc.	Kohlmeyer & Co.
Legg & Co.	Moore, Leonard & Lynch, Incorporated Nesbitt Thomson Securities, Inc.	Newhard, Cook & Co.
The Ohio Company	Prescott, Merrill, Turben & Co Reinholdt & Gardner	Singer, Deane & Scribner
Sutro & Co.		C. E. Unterberg, Towbin Co.

The 1969 announcement of the sale of beneficial shares in a trust that would evolve over the years into Urstadt Biddle Properties.

The timing of the new company's debut was felicitous. In the previous two years, the number of existing REITs had almost doubled, from 65 to 125; and an industry that a decade previously had gotten off to a slow and somewhat shaky start had begun to experience a boom. Over the next few years, REIT assets would increase from $1 billion to $20 billion.

HREI now had $92.5 million to invest in long-term investments for the portfolio that would provide a steady flow of dividends to shareholders. But while the whole idea of REITs was to provide liquidity for smaller investors who had previously shied away from real estate because it could not be bought and sold in small or large parcels at a moment's notice, the actual real estate deals that underlay the REIT, the creation of its portfolio of real estate investments, had to be done the old-fashioned way: painstakingly. Hubbard Real Estate Investments was the first major REIT specializing in the sale and leaseback of commercial and industrial properties. And these acquisitions took time and effort to negotiate and finalize. Even after the deals were done—and the Merrill Lynch-constituted advisor had some of them underway well before the board of trustees had its first meeting—they often could not be consummated until certain conditions had been met. For example, a deal might call for the REIT to buy and lease back a warehouse that was at the time under construction. But until it was finished or passed a certain stage of construction, no money would change hands.

The upshot was that HREI had more than $90 million that had to be put into short-term investments until those long-term investments were ready to proceed. The Trust's requirement for these short-term investments was that they offer maximum returns and safety along with sufficient liquidity so that the money would be available to complete the deal when the time came. HREI put $51 million into government obligations, $25 million into R. H. Macy mortgages, and $15 million into mortgages of the Fidelity Life Insurance Company. They would also eventually invest in mortgages of Vornado, a prominent real estate company, and of Bessemer Securities Corporation.

While it was temporarily parking its money at the most advantageous terms it could find, Hubbard Real Estate Investments began a very important tradition that has continued without interruption to this day. The board of trustees declared the Trust's first quarterly dividend: $0.35 a share, payable on January 15, 1970.

Building a Portfolio

The Merrill Lynch advisory body had drawn up a long-term investment plan for HREI that would spread its acquisitions out over two years. The advisor's choices would go far toward determining the Trust's early performance, and in the light of that, it might be tempting to speculate on how things might have gone in the Trust's early history had the acquisitions they considered but not made—with Xerox, Bethlehem Steel, and JCPenney—worked out. But that was the road not taken. Instead, the plan called for HREI to invest the bulk of the money from the stock offering in land and buildings now owned or being built by three corporations: Safeway Stores, W. T. Grant, and Chrysler.

Emblematic of HREI's initial operation was its $22 million purchase and leaseback of forty-one supermarkets from Safeway Stores. Everything about this deal was related to Merrill Lynch, which had brought the Safeway chain into being in the first place, when it presided over the 1926 merger of Skaggs Stores, founded in 1915 by a Baptist minister, and the Sam Seeling Stores that only recently had changed its name to "Safeway." In fact, Merrill Lynch not only had helped to create a retail behemoth of close to one thousand grocery stores in the mid-1920s, mostly in California and the Pacific Northwest, it had also taken a controlling interest in it. In succeeding years, Merrill Lynch arranged the financing for the chain's rapid expansion, which reached a peak of 3,527 stores in 1931. In later years the number of stores would shrink, but their size would increase. In 1955, Safeway chose as its new CEO Robert A. Magowan, a Merrill Lynch executive and son-in-law of Charles Merrill.

By the time that HREI became involved with the supermarket giant in 1970, Safeway had become an international chain, although its strength was still in the United States, predominantly west of the Mississippi. At the time of the sale and leaseback, Safeway was only three years away from surpassing A&P in sales to become the highest-grossing chain of supermarkets in the country.

While this particular venture was clearly in Merrill Lynch's interest, the bottom line was that it was, in fact, also in the interests of Hubbard Real Estate Investments' shareholders. Regardless of its Merrill Lynch connection, Safeway was a solid, profitable supermarket chain—about to become the biggest of its kind—and it fit the ideal profile for an HREI investment. The tenant was blue chip, ensuring that rents would be paid steadily and on time, bolstering the REIT's ability to pay steady dividends.

But the other two central components of HREI's initial portfolio, W. T. Grant and Chrysler, would turn out to be more problematic investments. Just as portfolio managers did not have the personal computers and easily accessible spreadsheets available today, neither did they have the hindsight of several decades of business history now available. In hindsight, Grant had internal problems related to its management philosophy and weakening position in its industry, and Chrysler was also in need of an infusion of new managerial talent. Chrysler would in addition run afoul of looming inflation.

W. T. Grant was at one time, like F. W. Woolworth's and S. S. Kresge, one of the dime store giants. Its large general merchandise stores were familiar sights in downtowns across America. Founded in 1906, the chain had well over one thousand outlets by the time that HREI invested in it through sale leasebacks.

But two problems were already eating away at Grant's foundation. Too few of the W. T. Grant stores were in the suburbs, which was increasingly where its customers and the large parking lots for their cars were. Compounding its problems, Grant's management, in the midst of the company's belated efforts to catch up with the competition and expand beyond its downtown base orientation, persisted in paying dividends, even when it had to borrow to do so. The HREI initial stake in this shaky empire was less than $3 million for one store and land for another, but would grow to $25 million in eleven facilities by the time the investment plan had been fully put into effect in 1972.

If Grant's problems might have begun to be visible to some observers in 1970, much of Chrysler's were still beyond the horizon at this point, although the company's recent history had been one in which its management had, with disturbing frequency, guessed wrong on what Americans wanted in their new automobiles. Nor had its inventory control been ideal. Too often, there was a mismatch between production line output and dealer demand, turning factory parking lots into unintended showcases for unsold cars. At least someone on the HREI Board of Trustees must have had some doubts about Chrysler, since it was the only company in the initial investment program about which a question was raised concerning its financial condition. Still, in 1970, Chrysler remained third in market share of America's most famous and beloved consumer product; and only a seer could have foreseen OPEC's turning off the oil spigot a few years later and the spike in gasoline prices and ruinous inflation that accompanied it. HREI's investment in Chrysler amounted to $13 million for seven of the auto manufacturer's warehouses.

Hubbard Real Estate Investments also purchased one hundred acres of land in Ohio, where Ashland Oil was building a divisional headquarters, and leased it back to Ashland. In California that first year, HREI also spent $4.5 million on a sale leaseback of a Broadway-Hale department store. And when depreciation unexpectedly freed up more money than it had allocated for acquisitions in 1970, the REIT bought and leased back an Alpha Beta Acme Markets supermarket in Sepulveda, California. The purchase price was $1.9 million.

The Relationship of the Board of Trustees to Its "Advisor"

It can't be overemphasized that it was the Trust's advisor, Hubbard, Westervelt, a subsidiary of HREI's sponsor, Merrill Lynch, that identified potential investment possibilities, negotiated with the principals of those possibilities, and completed the transactions—all functions that a REIT would today perform for itself. The function of HREI's board of trustees in helping to create a portfolio of investment properties was to sign off on the transactions initiated and consummated by the advisor. These real estate deals involved properties—land, warehouses, and retail facilities—all around America. The trustees were not able to inspect the locations before approving investments involving millions of dollars. For example, the minutes of the special meeting of the board of trustees of December 11, 1969, state—with reference to the Chrysler warehouses that were in the course of being acquired from the automotive giant prior to being leased back to Chrysler—that they "had been inspected by Real Estate Research Corporation from Chicago, which had given a favorable telephone summary and was forwarding reports on each property to the trust."

In fact, even a decade after HREI's formation, the trustees, if not flying completely blind, would still usually be making their final decisions without any firsthand knowledge of the properties involved. William F. Murdoch, Jr., who would later replace Ralph Coburn as HREI's president, recalled long after, "We had never seen many of our properties." They often lacked the most basic information, Murdoch said. "What happens in this town? Is there a lumberyard? Is there a college there? Is there a main street?"

It's not even clear to what extent the principals or employees of the advisor, Hubbard, Westervelt, were actually able to do onsite evaluations of what they were recommending for acquisition as long-term investments. More often than not, they appear to have also relied on the reports by local or regional firms that specialized in evaluating property.

At its worst, when this method of operation was combined with the sometimes-large number of significant properties involved, the whole operation could take on the character of a board game, in which pieces of property were moved around in an abstract fashion. In the Safeway deal, involving forty-one stores, for instance, the Trust rejected four of the stores at the last minute because of certain problems with their locations or tax complications involving particular units. Safeway responded by substituting four other stores, subject to the approval of the advisor and the board of trustees. The stores were located in two states, Texas and California, and were either completed or in various stages of construction. The Trust had to bring the total back up to forty-one, since it was required by the federal REIT law to invest a set amount of its capital in real estate and needed the leasebacks to provide the revenue that would fund dividends for shareholders. In less than two months, the advisors and the board had signed off on the substitutions, site unseen.

When it came to initiating acquisitions, the ball was in the advisor's court. Hubbard, Westervelt presented to the trustees the investment opportunities Hubbard had researched and followed through on, often to the point of negotiating a done deal lacking all but a closing. The advisor did not always keep the trustees informed about what might be in the hopper short of a deal. For example, at the meeting of March 1, 1973, the advisor informed the board that it was then looking into ten investment possibilities. But as the minutes stated, "none is sufficiently advanced to warrant presentation to the Trustees at this time."

But while the board of trustees mostly signed off on acquisitions presented to it by the Trust's advisor, it was by no means a rubber stamp. For example, in those early years, they rejected the purchase of a shopping mall in Saratoga, New York, and also turned down a bowling alley complex in Illinois because the "risk-reward ratio" was unsatisfactory.

The advisor also recommended the quarterly dividend, usually with not much argument from the trustees. An exception was in May 1973 when the advisor's suggestion that the dividend be raised to $0.39 a share elicited some opposition on the part of at least one trustee, who pointed out that in order to meet the increase, HREI might have to dip into the funds that would become available from depreciation, money usually earmarked for new investments. But after a discussion, the board agreed to the dividend increase.

The board did not automatically accept the value the advisor put on its own services. The board had to reapprove the use of the advisor's services and its fee every year. That fee was initially set at 4 percent of the Trust's gross income, less any fees the advisor collected from serving as a broker to the companies from which the Trust acquired property. For the first year, these fees entirely offset the 4 percent HREI would have owed its advisor. Nevertheless, in the fall of 1970, the board asked Hubbard, Westervelt to justify its advisory fee for the coming year with a detailed breakdown of everything it was doing for the REIT. In a September 17 letter to the board, Hubbard, Westervelt made (and won) its case: "Our services as Advisor covered short-term investments, SEC matters, reports to stockholders, stockholder inquiries, dividend distributions, New York Stock Exchange listing, banking relations, programming of funds, tax matters, appraisals, frequent visits to the Boston office, Trustees meetings and a myriad of services incident to the launching and daily operation of a sizeable trust with 26,000 stockholders."

The HREI Board of Trustees was sensitive to the issue of potential conflicts of interest involving its advisor. The structure of the REIT, in which the "advisor," as a part of Merrill Lynch, performed investment banking services for HREI *and* the company from which it was buying property was a minefield of potential conflict of interest. An added reason for caution—the board made clear—was the fact that Hubbard, Westervelt, its advisor, was also doing consulting work to the advisor of another REIT, Cousins Mortgage and Equity Investments. This was a topic of discussion at a special meeting of the HREI Trustees on August 31, 1970, where, nevertheless, the board decided that a conflict of interest did not exist.

Outside of the negative power it derived from giving or withholding its approval on major decisions that, in reality, had been made within the corporate confines of Merrill Lynch, the board of trustees initially had little power to influence the direction of Hubbard Real Estate Investments. Not that they didn't honestly try to find at least a few little ways to make the Trust run better. For example, at its meeting on December 6, 1972, the trustees adopted the money-saving measure of mailing out the annual report "without envelope" to cut down on the cost of postage. And in October 1973, the trustees discussed the possibility of "piggybacking" the notice of the annual shareholder's meeting and the proxy statement with the report.

The Initial Investment Program Fulfilled

In the fall of 1970, at the end of its first fiscal year, in its first annual report, Hubbard Real Estate Investments told shareholders that it was already "a substantial factor in the real estate trust field" and declared itself satisfied that it had "made substantial progress" toward its goal "to provide shareholders with reasonably assured, gradually increasing income, combined with potential for long-term capital appreciation." Dividends for the first year had added up to $1.42 a share, and net income was $6,216,434, or $1.55 a share. Depreciation was $352,536.

In its second year, the Trust paid out dividends of $1.46 a share. Net income per share was $1.62; and cash flow, net income plus depreciation, and other noncash charges was $1.92. Depreciation was just under $1 million, constituting funds that did not have to be paid out in dividends and could thus be used to make further acquisitions, increasing HREI's equity base.

With the launch of the Trust accomplished and the establishment of HREI as a going concern with long-term investments soon to hit the $90 million mark, the board of trustees augmented its membership and specialized its functions. In the summer of 1970, it hired Brinley M. Hall, a lawyer and friend of HREI president Ralph G. Coburn, to serve as treasurer and full-time administrator in its Boston office. In March 1971, well over a year after the Trust had commenced operations and officially begun to negotiate real estate transactions, Hall would tour some of the Trust's properties in western states, providing for the board its first extensive onsite, firsthand description of its properties in operation.

On December 1, 1971, the board set up a four-member Executive Committee, empowered to sign off on the investment of as much as $10 million of HREI's funds between regular board meetings. It also increased the number of members on the board from five to seven and immediately filled the new positions with John C. Hubbard and Brinley M. Hall. The board created an Audit Committee on May 23, 1972.

The Trust also began to act in concert with other REITs on matters of mutual concern. HREI had joined the National Association of Real Estate Investment

Trusts early on, at the end of 1969; and HREI's president, Ralph Coburn, became a member of its board of governors. Several times in those early years, HREI joined other REITs in pushing for legislation favorable to its industry. For example, in the fall of 1970, it contributed several thousand dollars to the campaign to induce New York State and New York City to alter their tax codes to make conditions more favorable for REITs doing business there.

In the summer of 1971, with its long-term investment program about two-thirds funded, the Trust was juggling its short-term investments, trying to have them mature precisely as the funds were needed for property acquisitions. What made this cash flow management a bit tricky was that payments were due to reimburse Grant and Ashland for construction costs when certain prescribed levels of construction were achieved. Given the nature of construction, those dates could not be precisely projected, so some borrowing was always possibly in the offing.

The NAREIT index debuted at the beginning of 1972, a manifestation of increased interest in REITs. This still relatively new form of real estate investment already had enough of a history and a sufficient number of companies for investors and brokers to need tools with which they could track REIT performance. One of those REITs, HREI, was doing quite well. It completed the investment program set out for it by its advisor on schedule in 1972, ending the fiscal year with sixty-six properties. It paid out $1.49 per share in dividends based on a $2.07 per share cash flow, up from the previous year. Total depreciation since the Trust had been launched now topped $3 million, funding yet more investments to increase the Trust's equity base. During the year, the Trust had instituted an automatic dividend reinvestment service for its shareholders.

A new acquisition the following year was land on which International Harvester had built truck facilities. In 1973, HREI also invested in a mortgage on a Rich's department store in North Carolina, with the intention of making more such loans to the company. The investment involved a relatively small sum of less than $150,000 at the favorable terms of twenty-five years at 9 percent. At the time the advisor viewed it as a "pilot project," possibly "a prototype for future investments." The trustees, however, were not entirely sure they wanted to fly this route in the future, expressing some concern that the store leased rather than owned its land.

The Trust now owned department stores, supermarkets, company headquarters, and storage and distribution facilities located throughout the country, although the area of greatest concentration was in the Southwest. At its meeting on December 3, 1970, the trustees, at the suggestion of HREI's advisor, even seriously considered becoming a sponsor of a thirty-two-acre middle-income housing development in New York City, should the tax laws in the City and in New York State become more REIT-friendly. Developer Sam LeFrak, whose enormous Lefrak City housing development in Queens was not far from the proposed project, was a player in this planned development. The project, which came up at several board meetings, was called Willow Lake Village, to be located over the railroad yards near Flushing Meadows, the former site of two world's fairs. It would be built under the State's Mitchell-Lama law, which offered limited profits and a tax break to developers who agreed to cap rents over a set period of time, after which the project could withdraw from the program and the apartments be rented at market rates. Although the advisor and the board eventually passed on it, the proposal was significant for the REIT's future in one important respect. In considering it, the Hubbards consulted then New York State commissioner of the Division of Housing and Community Renewal, Charles J. Urstadt, marking Urstadt's first contact of any kind with the company he would one day lead as its CEO.

HREI was thus virtually all over the map in the types of property it owned and considered owning. But geographically all of the properties the Trust owned, no matter what type they were, had one thing in common: not one of them was located near the people who were making or approving the decision to buy them. All were managed and leased by local property management companies, not by HREI or its advisor.

Inflation

In the fall of 1971, the trustees were momentarily uncertain about whether real estate investment trusts came under the regulation of President Nixon's ninety-day wage-price freeze and the economic controls that would follow, which he had announced in August. For example, could HREI raise dividends without running afoul of the new policy? It could, it was advised. But the Trust could not get an immediate answer about whether tax escalation clauses in some of its leases (to reimburse HREI in future years when its real estate taxes on the leased property increased) would be permitted. In hindsight, we know that a greater worry should have been the underlying inflation that the president felt had necessitated the freeze in the first place. Under its sale-leaseback approach to investing, HREI depended on relatively low inflation to make an essentially fixed return on its investments work. Inflation was not only picking up steam, but would soon receive an enormous boost from the OPEC nations when they clamped down on the flow of oil through Middle Eastern pipelines.

For the real estate industry, inflation meant most of all higher interest rates. Companies would have to pay more to borrow, and businesses and consumers seeking mortgages would be hit hard in the pocketbook as well. All of that spelled contraction. HREI was partly insulated from the worst that inflation could bring. Unlike the mortgage REITs that had pioneered the new real estate investment trust format in the 1960s, HREI was based on equity investments. The Trust held a relatively small amount of short-term mortgages when the rates began to rise appreciably. In fact, the rate increase actually benefited HREI, which began to get a better return on its short-term investments. Hubbard had also avoided any extensive borrowing itself, funding its investments mostly from the proceeds of its stock sale and from cash flow.

Hubbard was also growing increasingly wary of acquiring properties that were overpriced in a market that was becoming overheated. At the board's special meeting on March 9, 1972, G. M. Hubbard of the Trust's advisor spoke to that issue. According to the minutes of that meeting, he told the trustees that some REITs "appear to be taking on inferior merchandise at relatively high prices." Hubbard Real Estate Investments would not be tempted to take that path.

By resisting the temptation to grow simply for the sake of growth, and because it had been especially prudent in avoiding debt, Hubbard Real Estate Investments was in a better place than were most other REITs as turbulence hit the economy in the early and mid-1970s. On August 21, 1973, John Hubbard told the board that "under prevailing economic conditions" in the REIT industry, HREI should be looking at the possibilities of acquiring other REITs "or some of their properties" at favorable prices. At that same meeting, Hubbard also reviewed the effect of "ever-increasing short-term interest rates on current investment opportunities."

On December 4, 1973, Ralph Coburn, according to the minutes of the trustee's meeting, "called the attention of the Trustees to a listing of some 40 REITs contained in their folders, which have experienced or reported declines in earnings on recent dates." He pointed out that the high cost of short-term borrowing especially had hit REITs specializing in construction and development loans. Two weeks later, the board was considering the possibility of authorizing a preferred stock offering to be used to buy properties from REITs that had to trim or liquidate their portfolios because of hard times.

HREI's balance sheet would have been envied by many REITs in 1973. Its liabilities were just over $2 million; it had undistributed net income of over $1.3 million; and with its sixty-six leased properties earning a net income per share of $1.55, it paid out $1.54 per share in dividends. In its annual report, the Trust called the year "satisfactory." Whether the wide geographic dispersal of its properties could be characterized in the same way was a matter of opinion. A map in the report showed the location of HREI's properties stretching from Massachusetts through the Mid-Atlantic States and the Midwest and then down through the South and Southwest until it curved up in an arc along the West Coast all the way to the state of Washington. As Charles J. Urstadt was later to observe with less satisfaction, "it looked like they were trying to color in a map of the whole country."

Nothing ever came of the idea that HREI might acquire properties or other REITs at a fire sale caused by the sharp upward thrust of interest rates. In July 1974, with the OPEC tightening of the oil spigots having taken its toll on the American economy, HREI found it necessary to send its shareholders a brief report acknowledging the difficult business conditions caused by "high short-term interest rates, inflation, and shortages of energy and materials," but reassuring them that HREI itself was in no danger.

Ralph G. Coburn, first president of Hubbard Real Estate Investments.

William F. Murdoch, Jr., who became the Trust's second president in 1975. He held that position until 1989, when Charles J. Urstadt succeeded him.

The K-Mart store in Fall River, Massachusetts occupied a space formerly filled by a branch of the bankrupt Grants chain.

A Safeway store in North Richland Hills, Texas. Emblematic of HREI's initial operation was its $22 million purchase and lease back of 41 supermarkets from Safeway Stores.

Trouble on the Horizon

In the short run, HREI could ride out a spike in interest rates, but its tenants' balance sheets were another matter. Stable dividend payouts were based on a stable cash flow, and that in turn depended on tenants prospering and at least being able to stay in business at the locations for which they had long-term leases. Should they go under and have to break their leases, the Trust would be left with at least temporarily nonperforming assets. Anything that disrupted lessee stability would spell eventual trouble for the landlord, and trouble lay not too far ahead.

In its July 1974 report to shareholders, HREI had to acknowledge what its shareholders had begun to read in the financial press: W. T. Grant, a mainstay of the Trust's investment portfolio—to the tune of a book value of $25,285,000, the annualized revenue from which was $2,480,000—was floundering. The Trust conceded in the report that the giant variety store's financial data was "disappointing," but reassured its shareholders that tenant delinquencies remained at or below the industry average.

The Trust's annual report for 1974 elaborated on this situation, which was becoming a matter of increasing concern. In his letter to shareholders in the report, HREI president Ralph Coburn stated: "During the past year inflation, tight money and high interest rates have combined to sharply constrict construction activity, and many of the same factors have created strong pressures on real estate investment trusts." He reiterated that under the circumstances, Hubbard was doing quite well—it had paid dividends of $1.58 per share, up from the previous year—but acknowledged that the darkening clouds in the economy were creating rough weather for HREI tenants. He pointed out that "Grant is experiencing serious financial difficulties and the industry wide slump in new car sales has adversely affected Chrysler."

Grant had become a problem for HREI in a different form eighteen months earlier. Nine of the ten stores that Grant leased from HREI—an eleventh location, in Albany, Georgia, was a warehouse—were part of retail complexes, if not actual shopping centers. Grant's lease on the tenth store, in Richmond, Indiana, required that a supermarket locate next to the facility by a certain date; otherwise Grant would have to buy back the store from HREI.

At their meeting in February 1973, the trustees discussed a report from their advisor that the big chain was concerned about the Richmond, Indiana, location. It was doing well, according to Grant, but the chain thought it might be vulnerable to the possible construction nearby of a "full-blown shopping center." Grant wanted to develop the area surrounding its store—which it would have to do anyway, according to the terms of its lease—but didn't have the experience or the personnel to do this itself; it would have to bring in an outside developer.

This issue resurfaced in several future board meetings as discussions between Grant and HREI about the possible alteration of the Richmond location dragged on, with HREI granting extensions of the deadline by which a supermarket had to be developed next to the store. When it arose at the meeting of January 22, 1974, the board members noted in passing Grant's "recent unsatisfactory earnings reports." Four months later, on May 21, Grant's overall condition was being treated as a looming crisis at HREI's board of trustees meeting. Coburn told the trustees that he had discussed the situation with a Merrill Lynch analyst and that John Hubbard had been visiting the stores Grant leased from HREI. In fact, several trustees had been doing some fact-finding of their own with top Grant executives.

With HREI president Ralph Coburn due to retire shortly at this possibly critical juncture in the Trust's relatively short history, this seemed like a good time to gradually introduce Coburn's successor to what would possibly become his first and biggest headache on the job. At the May 21 meeting, Coburn informed the trustees that he was bringing aboard as a Merrill Lynch Hubbard vice president William F. Murdoch, Jr., who had "a considerable background in real estate." Murdoch would join Coburn in a detailed examination of the status of all eleven locations that Grant leased from HREI.

Murdoch was then president of Schroder Real Estate Corporation, a subsidiary of J. Henry Schroder Banking Corporation of New York. A 1952 Princeton graduate with an MBA degree from Harvard, Murdoch had worked for marketing consultants Booz Allen Hamilton, and the Rouse real estate development company in Maryland. He had become a vice president of the real estate subsidiary of Eastman Dillon Union Securities & Co. and had held that position until he joined Schroder in 1970. Coburn told the trustees that Murdoch would succeed him as president of the Trust upon his retirement in 1975. Murdoch was to serve in that position for the next fourteen years.

Grant, failing to develop the land next to its Richmond store, finally had to buy it back from HREI at its original purchase price, as per the terms of its lease. But at this point, Grant's troubles were cascading, and what to do with its Richmond location was hardly its most pressing problem. The company had just reported an annual loss of $175 million. Unfortunately, as 1975 began, Grant's problems were also Hubbard Real Estate Investments' problems. The potential loss of HREI's $2,480,000 annual revenue from its Grant properties was a very serious matter. Without that revenue, the Trust's dividend was in danger. What's more, under the bankruptcy laws, should Grant file for bankruptcy it would have the right to reject all of its HREI leases, with a cap on damages that the landlord could collect of three years rent, and these potential damages would be unsecured.

Typical of companies in trouble, Grant announced cost reduction measures, closing some smaller and less profitable stores; but the crisis had gone beyond correction with small measures. Early in 1975, Grant announced that it would shut down sixty-six of its retail locations, including two stores rented from HREI in Erie, Pennsylvania, and San Jose, California. In October came the announcement that the company filed for bankruptcy.

The turbulence stirred up by the bankruptcy of its biggest tenant, which represented about 27 percent of its portfolio and a third of its rental income, was causing waves at HREI. At the board meeting on October 21, the Trust's legal counsel cautioned the board against insider trading during the crisis. HREI's share price was experiencing unusual fluctuations; and as advised by counsel, "insiders should remain on the sidelines, since, despite all efforts to make proper disclosures of material facts, changes are occurring so rapidly that at any given moment insiders are or may be in possession of certain facts that will not be known to the investing public."

On November 1, 1975, *Forbes* discussed HREI's heavy exposure in the Grant collapse, noting that the REIT's share price had hit a new low of $9. The magazine article indicated that HREI president William F. Murdoch's belief that the Trust would weather the storm and even come out ahead might have been a sunny spin he was putting on some rather-dark tidings for his company. But the piece also acknowledged that the situation could represent an opportunity for HREI, since the Grant leases had been negotiated five years previously, before steep inflation rates had changed so many business plans, and that now the Trust could bring in new tenants at more favorable rents. Besides, unlike so many other REITs, Hubbard Real Estate Investments primarily owned buildings, not mortgages; the Trust was not drowning in debt.

Actually, Murdoch was not just putting on a happy face for the press. The Grant debacle was, in fact, a calamity concealing an opportunity; and Murdoch and his associates at the Trust's advisor were determined to exploit the opening.

The Grant Bankruptcy Has a Silver Lining for HREI

Recalling those days, Murdoch would later state: "We could have turned over the entire Grant portfolio to a broker, but they would have just put their signs out there and called a few people. Instead, we studied every situation with a goal of maximizing the value to Hubbard. Given the large size of the Grant stores—over 100,000 square feet each—we could readily identify the limited number of possible tenants. Then we focused on them and contacted the right people. It was a critical job for us and we focused on it every day."

Indeed, within a month of publication of the *Forbes* article, HREI had leased the former Grant stores in Citrus Heights, California, and Drayton Plains, Michigan, to the S. S. Kresge Company which intended to reopen them as Kmarts. The Trust's "biggest risk" from the Grant bankruptcy, as Murdoch phrased it—the 473,000-square-foot warehouse property in Albany, Georgia, located in an industrial park—was also quickly leased. Morry Hubbard of the Trust's advisor had flown down to Georgia to survey the scene and had noted a nearby Firestone Tire & Rubber facility. In short order, he had a made a deal with Firestone for the warehouse; and Firestone took occupancy on March 1, 1976. The lease for Firestone was advantageous because it would not show up on its books as a loan, thereby allowing it to expand without incurring debt. In reality, Firestone had indeed borrowed. It had a net lease with HREI; but under the terms of the deal, at the end of the lease, Firestone would own the property.

The two stores plus the warehouse accounted for about 30 percent of HREI's Grant exposure. But its early success in filling these locations did not mean that Hubbard was home free. Realistically, it could take as much as three years to lease all of the Grant stores, and that offered the disturbing prospect of some significant nonperforming assets.

On December 9, 1975, the trustees approved the $6.5 million reserve that its advisor wanted to set aside to cover losses and carrying charges associated with the Grant problem. They also signed off on a quarterly dividend of $0.30, a drop of 25 percent from the previous quarter. The Trust also took advantage of new federal regulations governing REITs that now permitted them to directly manage for up to ninety days property taken back due to a bankruptcy. On December 18, the board approved the hiring of Sanford Goldstein—an independent contractor who specialized in property management, development, and brokerage services—at a fee of $1,300 a month that would later rise to $2,500 plus expenses, to market the Erie, Pennsylvania, store that had been vacated by Grant. And in February 1976, the Trust began to pay Hubbard Property Management, a subsidiary of its advisor, $27,500 a month to perform the same services for the remainder of the Grant locations.

By the summer of 1976, Hubbard Property Management had filled the former Fall River and Springfield, Massachusetts, Grant stores with Kmart and Caldor units. The Trust had also leased the Manassas, Virginia, location to Hecht's, a division of May Department Stores. At the end of 1976, HREI filed a suit to recover the $4,162,000 it figured to lose from expenses related to the Grant failure; but nobody was optimistic about recovering that amount.

While the W. T. Grant situation brought some unwelcome publicity, substantial legal expenses, a dent in the Trust's revenues and a temporary drop in its dividend, it also showed HREI's ability to weather a storm and come out, if anything, all the better for it. For the new leases negotiated with the tenants that replaced Grant were mostly less bondlike and finally began to resemble more traditional real estate transactions. The Trust now had some responsibility for maintenance of its properties. There was some provision for rent increases over the course of the lease, accounting for inflation, which had become a disturbing trend in the decade that was only half over. There were also provisions in some of the leases for rent increases based on sales volume. And when leases were renewed, the new rents would no longer be of the step-down variety, but would rather ascend, as one might expect them to do in a real estate business.

The company acknowledged in its 1975 annual report that it had been "a challenging period" for HREI. "The problems of the W. T. Grant Company came to a head toward the end of Fiscal 1975," Coburn admitted to shareholders. "And as a result of a substantial reserve, the financial statements of Hubbard Real Estate Investments show a loss of $353,383 for the year." Coburn went on to put the Grant problems in perspective, noting that the Trust was otherwise doing fine and would be back on track once all of the vacated Grant locations had been leased to new tenants. Even more reassuring to shareholders must have been the $1.60 per share dividend for that year, up slightly over the previous year.

A New Trustee

Dealing with the W. T. Grant situation and leasing its now vacant stores was the most dramatic story of this period in the Trust's history. But what was going on in the background would ultimately leave a bigger mark on Hubbard Real Estate Investments.

At its meeting on October 15, 1974, the members of HREI's board of trustees discussed the need for some new and younger blood at the Trust. Richard Willis, one of the board's four original independent members not connected to Merrill Lynch, had resigned in the spring. To replace him, HREI would seek someone no older than his mid-40s who had extensive real estate experience. Housing and office space were investment areas that the advisors were increasingly considering, so the new trustee ought to have expertise in those fields.

At the beginning of 1975, the board of trustees was expanded to nine members; and one of them was the younger trustee the board had been seeking—Charles J. Urstadt, former commissioner of Housing and Community Renewal of the State of New York, then founding chairman and chief executive officer of the Battery Park City Authority, the body created to fill in and select developers for a hundred-acre landfill site in the Hudson River off the southern tip of Manhattan. This was billed as the largest office and residential development complexes in the United States. Urstadt had become a public figure by dint of his leadership in this huge and complicated joint government-private business venture and through his service as New York State's commissioner of Housing and Community Renewal and chairman of the New York State Housing Finance Agency. Urstadt had also been instrumental in creating the New York State Urban Development Corporation, later renamed the Empire State Development Corporation.

New York State's Governor Nelson A. Rockefeller had chosen a thoroughly experienced real estate man for these daunting jobs. Other boys growing up in the Bronx in the 1920s and 1930s might have hoped to be a baseball player or fireman, but Urstadt had always known he wanted to work in real estate. His grandfather, who had invested in apartment buildings in the Bronx in the 1920s, and Charles' father, an engineer who had come into his father's business, used to take young Charles when they visited the buildings to collect the rents, showing the boy the importance of paying attention to detail.

Urstadt graduated from the renowned Bronx High School of Science at the tender age of sixteen and then obtained his BA and MBA degrees at Dartmouth—where he was an all-American swimmer—and earned a law degree at Cornell. After a stint in the US Navy, he joined the universally recognized real estate firm of Webb & Knapp, where he worked under the legendary real estate developer William Zeckendorf for six years. There Urstadt participated in major deals involving properties ranging from New York's famed Chrysler Building to the Twentieth Century Fox Studios. When Webb & Knapp passed to Alcoa in 1963, Urstadt went along, becoming vice president of Alcoa Residences, the corporation's real estate subsidiary. It was from there that Governor Rockefeller tapped him for the State Housing and Community Renewal, Battery Park City, and other housing assignments.

Urstadt, after leaving the Battery Park City Authority at the end of 1978, would become chairman and president of Pearce, Urstadt, Mayer & Greer, Inc., a diversified real estate brokerage, finance, and development company in New York City.

Urstadt's first board meeting and formal introduction to the Trust and its members was on April 8, 1975, at the Federal Club in Boston, where he was immediately elected to HREI's Executive Committee. Also at that meeting, William F. Murdoch formally succeeded Ralph Coburn as president of the Trust. George M. Hubbard, Jr., had retired as chairman of the advisor, since renamed Merrill Lynch Hubbard, on January 1 and had been named a trustee.

Real estate developer Martin Cleary also joined the board. Cleary had been a senior vice president for mortgages and real estate with the Teachers Insurance and Annuity Association of America and headed the prominent Cleveland real estate developer Jacobs, Visconsi & Jacobs.

In May, the advisor—which at the beginning of 1974 had changed its named from Hubbard, Westervelt & Mottelay to Merrill Lynch Hubbard—added Stephen C. Hagen to work with Murdoch. Hagen had been with Connecticut General Life Insurance Company (now CIGNA) where he was head of Asset Management for an equity real estate portfolio. Hagen had also worked at the Rouse Company where he managed its commercial properties. Also now prominent in the management of the Trust's advisor was James L. Mooney.

Diversifying the Portfolio

HREI's new approach in its search for investment opportunities had become clear when the board convened on January 22, 1975. As has been pointed out, the advisor ordinarily presented to board members only proposed investments that were already well on their way to becoming acquisitions. However, on that day, they put before the trustees a number of possibilities that they were first considering in order to get a sense of the "present investment criteria which the Trustees would require of any investment submitted for their approval." Clearly the advisor was trying to feel its way through previously uncharted waters. Among the possibilities being considered, the minutes of the meeting reveal, were "multi-tenant office buildings, shopping centers, restaurants, apartment buildings and a motel, that these properties generally were mortgaged, some were leaseholds only, and that, whereas they offered the Trust an opportunity to invest in leveraged projects, an investment in any of these properties would constitute a departure from the Trust's present net lease portfolio."

At a meeting on January 30, 1975, the trustees turned down an investment in a bank building in downtown Las Vegas, concerned that the resort industry upon which the city's economy was based was too vulnerable to the then shaky economy. They did approve the purchase of a medical office building, but that acquisition ultimately fell through when a doctor whose practice was in the building bought the property.

In the spring of 1975, the Trust was looking into the possibility of investing in a large suburban Philadelphia apartment house and office buildings in Denver, Colorado, and Houston, Texas. The Houston property became a reality in June. At the trustee's meeting on June 19, the advisor presented them with a twenty-eight-page brochure on the building. Murdoch and Hagen had already inspected it and offered the opinion that the city had "a remarkable ability to absorb new office space." A local appraiser assured them that the $3.5 million they intended to commit was reasonable. The trustees approved.

"General conditions in the real estate industry during the past three years have been the worst in modern times," HREI solemnly declared in its annual report to shareholders in 1976. And this time, the $1.20 per share dividend, a considerable drop from the previous year's $1.60, served as an exclamation mark and reminder that, because of the Grant reserve, HREI was not entirely above the battle.

On the plus side, five of the eleven Grant locations had been leased by the end of the 1976 fiscal year; and on the whole, the leases were on better terms for the Trust than they had been with Grant. Especially important were provisions for rent increases, either at periodic intervals or with rising sales volume.

Over the next year, the trustees would approve sale-leaseback deals at former Grant locations in Tempe and Mesa, Arizona, where Mervyns, a California department store chain that would later be purchased by Dayton Hudson, opened department stores. The leases ran for twenty years and provided for rent increases, depending on sales volume. During this same period, Federated Department Stores would replace the Grant San Jose, California, location with a Gold Circle Store.

Kmart would ultimately take a total of four former Grant locations, all of which would pay escalated rents as business improved. HREI president Murdoch would later recall that the then-burgeoning discounter "wanted to blanket every metropolitan market in the country with stores every four miles." Initially Kmart insisted on the step-down renewal rents that had been part of the Grant leases, the terms of which had been public information. "They all love what you got before," Murdoch noted. But HREI let Kmart know that in the present improving commercial real estate leasing environment, the Trust could do better. The Erie, Pennsylvania, location was the toughest sell because, as Murdoch acknowledged, it had "limited traffic and modest income levels." When Kmart finally went for that location, the former HREI head recalled, "We celebrated."

Meanwhile, Hubbard had been upgrading its Safeway properties. Safeway bought back and closed its store in Santa Maria, California, located in a neighborhood in financial decline. The supermarket chain also bought back its store in Redmond, Washington. In Houston, HREI's office building was fully leased.

If investors needed guidance as to HREI's prospects only two years after its brush with disaster, they could have consulted *Value Line*. In the summer of 1977, that publication, trusted by millions to evaluate a company's outlook, called Hubbard Real Estate Investments "a choice investment for high current income and the likelihood of further dividend growth to 1980-82." The magazine optimistically foresaw the Trust earning $1.82 a share and paying the same amount in dividends by the end of that period. In fact, it was a bit too conservative. HREI's balance sheet would show net income per share of $1.88 and dividends per share of $1.21 in 1977, $1.82 and $1.35 in 1978, $2.15 and $1.62 in 1979, $1.90 and $1.79 in 1980, and $2.16 and $2.00 in 1981. In 1982, at the end of the range of *Value Line*'s estimate, HREI would earn $1.94 per share and pay out a dividend of $2.00 a share.

If investors were concerned about the Grant matter and worried about HREI's then-current exposure to Chrysler's woes, they needn't have been. The publication rated Hubbard "above average" for safety and evaluated the Trust's financial strength as the highest of all the REITs whose performance it followed. *Value Line* concluded: "Hubbard has weathered the worst real estate industry recession since the 1930s and had its largest lessee declared bankrupt; yet it made only a 25% dividend reduction and earnings will probably reach a new peak before the decade is over."

Meanwhile the Trust continued to investigate new investment opportunities. It considered the possibility of purchasing three hundred acres of land on Hayden

Island, between Portland, Oregon, and Vancouver, Washington, but nothing came of it. Nor was that as far west as HREI might be willing to go. In March 1978, the trustees signed off on the advisor's suggestion that for $3.6 million HREI add to its portfolio a condo beachfront development on the island of Maui, Hawaii. But two months later, that deal was off "because of the developer's unwillingness to pay current rates for mortgage money," according to the board minutes.

By the end of fiscal 1978, Hubbard Real Estate Investments had put most of its Grant troubles behind it. Its annual report began to sport a new and more appealing look. In 1978, for the first time, it was rich with color photographs of its holdings. The report took third place in the Best of Industry Annual Report Awards, sponsored by *Financial World*. Color was also returning to the real estate market, replacing the pallor of the earlier part of the decade. This was not an unmitigated blessing, since it meant there was greater competition for new acquisitions that would expand Hubbard's portfolio. "In this kind of market," the Trust told shareholders, it has "been unwilling to pay the prices demanded for prime property."

There was a story behind that sudden splash of color in the annual report. As previously noted, the trustees usually evaluated potential investments based solely on material handed to them by their advisor. Often they were not all that familiar even with the appearance of the properties in question. The same held true for properties already in the REIT's portfolio. In 1978, they decided to remedy that situation. As Murdoch later remembered it, "the Board decided that it would be desirable if someone could go to each property and give a detailed report about each one. So we hired my daughter Molly and paid her, I think, fifteen cents a mile, fifty dollars a property, and a reimbursement for her living expenses and film costs."

Molly, a college student, subcontracted some of the tasks involved to her fifteen-year-old brother who accompanied her. According to Molly, their job at each location was to photograph and map it, get information from the local chamber of commerce, check the sales volume, and talk to the store manager. Such was an important source of business intelligence for the board of trustees of the Hubbard Real Estate Investment Trust in the late 1970s.

The two intrepid travelers logged six thousand miles in Molly's Volkswagen, camping out along the way. Their father's only complaint afterward was that the Volkswagen got into too many of the images.

The prolonged Grant matter formally came to an end at the beginning of 1979 when Meijer, a combined supermarket discount store competitor of Kmart, leased the 133,000 square feet that the failed chain had occupied in Sterling Heights, Michigan, a northern suburb of Detroit.

Perhaps symbolic of change in HREI, 1979 also saw the addition of James O. York to the board. York had retired as president of R. H. Macy's Properties, the department store subsidiary in which HREI had made a short-term investment in its early years. But he had no connection to Hubbard's Dartmouth. Nevertheless he was an able man who fit in nicely with the other members and a valuable addition to the REIT.

Chrysler

What of Chrysler, the other problem in the Trust's portfolio in the early 1970s? After all, the huge auto manufacturer accounted for $1,687,000 of HREI's annual revenues and 21 percent of the Trust's assets. For 1974 and 1975, Chrysler was, as Murdoch was later to put it, "on life support"; it was bleeding some very highly publicized red ink. One could almost feel some of it dripping on the seven HREI warehouses it occupied. The term "plant closings" had become a staple of just about every story dealing with Chrysler. "We don't like to speculate about the worst," Murdoch told *Barron's* in April 1976; but he acknowledged, "We do think about it."

Unlike the situation with Grant, the lesser crisis involving Chrysler would drag on for many years. A possible Chrysler bankruptcy came up at the board of trustees meeting on September 14, 1979, and again at the meeting on December 4. At the March 11, 1980, meeting, the advisor's Stephen C. Hagen reported that a broker at Merrill Lynch Realty had mentioned to him the possibility of arranging, for a 3 percent commission, the sale of three of the automaker's HREI warehouses, an offer the trustees were willing to consider if they could get book value for the properties.

HREI began to shed part of its Chrysler exposure in July 1980 when the trustees formally authorized the sale of Chrysler's Pittsburgh warehouse. The auto company had stopped using it, although it had remained current on its rent for the facility. HREI took back its lease and sold the property to Westinghouse for $3.3 million in cash. According to HREI's annual report for 1981, "the transaction produced a $200,000 gain for financial reporting purposes, and a $700,000 gain for tax purposes."

HREI also found some new wiggle room when it came to the Trust's relationship with its troubled tenant. What they could do as Chrysler's landlord was to offer it an incentive to give better lease terms to HREI than the long-term fixed rents with step-down renewal rents its advisor had negotiated just a few years before. The carrot for Chrysler was an opportunity to improve its much-battered current cash flow. The Trust agreed to pay Chrysler $1 million to give up its rights to land adjacent to several of its HREI locations. Hubbard anticipated either selling the parcels at a later date or putting up new buildings on that land. In return, Chrysler agreed to lease changes involving renewal rents that would potentially add up to tens of millions of dollars for HREI.

The bottom line, as Murdoch later put it: "Chrysler survived and we got those rents."

Chapter Three

YEARS OF TRANSITION: THE 1980S

In the mid-1970s, some publications were questioning Hubbard Real Estate Investments' ability to survive the W. T. Grant bankruptcy. Not only did it survive, but by the early 1980s, the former Grant locations had been quickly leased to new tenants at better terms. The reserve set aside to allow for expenses involved with retenanting the Grant locations, which had temporarily skewed the Trust's balance sheet late in the decade, with net income taking a hit, was no longer necessary. This felicitous turn of events had even allowed HREI to pay out its highest dividend yet, $1.62 a share, in 1979.

Having survived an unexpectedly turbulent first decade, two themes would be prominent in the development of HREI in the first half of the 1980s: a further evolution in the makeup of its portfolio and the changing relationship between the Trust and its advisor.

By the mid-1970s, the Trust had already begun to break away from its original plan of sticking almost exclusively to sale and leaseback deals with step-down rents for lease renewals. No longer content to operate as if it were creating a bondlike product, HREI had taken on at least some aspects of a true real estate business, with potential growth and equity as well as stable fixed income now the criteria for selecting investments. The extreme inflation of the early 1970s alone would have guaranteed some movement away from its initial operation model. The unanticipated need to dispose of the former Grant leases provided the opportunity to structure new leases with new tenants who would now agree to pay increases over the course of the lease, often geared to their sales figures. In this new business model, lease renewals would bring with them higher rents, as is normal in real estate.

In its 1980 annual report, the Trust formally declared that it intended to focus on investments with "fewer fixed income characteristics." As the decade began, about half of the Hubbard portfolio consisted of fixed income types of properties. Moving further into growth-oriented investments would require great care. The task of selecting investments that offered the Trust good value was made more difficult not only by steady inflation, at least into the first few years of the decade, but also by new capital flowing into US real estate from abroad, particularly from Britain. This inflow of foreign capital helped to bid up the price of good properties. Syndicated limited partnerships, with their ability to pass through tax losses, also competed with REITs for available capital, pushing up the cost of borrowing.

New forms of ownership were also characteristic of the Trust's investments. Hubbard Real Estate Investments would now seek to own properties outright outside of the sale-leaseback mode of operation. It would be open to the purchase of office properties using leverage. It would also move into a few joint ventures. Each took it further away from something resembling a stock mutual fund and brought it a bit closer to a more typical real estate operation.

Along with the change in the financial terms of the new leases, HREI also began to negotiate leases that were somewhat more complex in terms of the landlord's responsibility in regard to its properties, moving away from the net leases that had characterized the Trust's business operations from its beginnings. Some of the burden of property upkeep, repairs, and insurance now fell on the Trust's shoulders, whereas before they had been borne solely by the tenant. Still prevented by law from hands-on management of its properties, HREI would have to hire local management companies to do the job.

The 1981 annual report boiled down the Trust's new strategy to "three elements: (1) to invest in operating properties where shorter leases can be re-written at higher rents as they expire, (2) to renegotiate fixed income leases where possible, and (3) to sell some net leased properties."

Diversification

In its investment program, large retail stores, shopping centers, and warehouses continued to be mainstays of the Trust, as in its early years. For example, for about $2.5 million in 1979, it added a ninety-three-thousand-square-foot office and warehouse complex in Newington, New Hampshire, and expanded it three years later with several acres of adjoining land. Early in 1980, HREI was considering for possible acquisition a Galesburg, Illinois, mall and warehouses in Iowa and Illinois, although they didn't pan out.

The REIT's investment program also reflected trends then percolating through the real estate industry as a whole. The buzz word was "diversification." Beginning in the mid-1970s and accelerating in the early 1980s, HREI was willing to look at almost anything anywhere in the United States that promised a good return. The exception was residential property, which the advisor had occasionally considered among legitimate investment possibilities in the 1970s. Several members of the board of directors in the early 1980s had had bad experiences with investments in apartment buildings, diminishing the place of that path in the Trust's investment pattern.

Office buildings now looked particularly attractive. With the rise in importance of the service and information industries in the American economy, office construction had become a hot market, one into which the Trust began to buy. As the Trust explained in the 1981 annual report, "office employment has grown faster than employment in other sectors of the economy and has pushed rents up rapidly, making office investment profitable."

Hubbard Real Estate Investments' Board of Trustees in 1980. From left to right: George M. "Morry" Hubbard, Jr, George T. Conklin, Jr., Charles J. Urstadt, William F. Murdoch, Jr., James O. York, Brinley M. Hall and John C. Hubbard. The Hubbards, in conjunction with Merrill Lynch, founded the Trust.

The Giffels Office Building in Southfield, Michigan, acquired in 1984. It would remain one of the REIT's non-core properties until its sale in 2005.

HREI had been a participant in ownership of a multitenant office building in Houston near the prominent Galleria development since 1975. Now its advisor suggested a joint venture on an energy-efficient, ten-story Portland, Oregon, office property where the developer, Prendergast & Associates, was about to begin construction. The first three floors of the structure would contain retail space and parking. The Union Pacific Railroad would eventually be the building's main tenant, occupying 204,000 square feet. The trustees signed off on the investment in the summer of 1979 in what was called the "1515 Building." HREI financed its contribution to the partnership, which the REIT would eventually control, with a first mortgage from a life insurance company at a relatively low rate.

In February 1981, it was One Denver Highlands, a 120,000-square-foot office building in suburban Denver, with adjacent land slated for possible further office development in an area that the annual report described as having possibly "the strongest economy in the nation." Six months later, when anticipated financing for that building could not be had on favorable terms, the board agreed to up HREI's participation in the transaction from $2.5 to a possible $12 million in equity and debt financing. The Denver venture was a partnership that HREI controlled.

A 50 percent partnership in an existing Charlotte, North Carolina, office building, for about $5.4 million, was another addition to the portfolio in 1981. The Trust anticipated that the city's planned infrastructure improvements in the area and a projected hotel and office complex across the street would add value to the building. The current below market rents had created the likelihood of increased cash flow from the building in the future as new leases were negotiated.

But hot as the office market was, there were already some clouds on the horizon. The 1982 annual report acknowledged that "the new projects in Portland, Oregon and Denver, Colorado are leasing more slowly than we expected, but they are doing well in the context of their respective markets." Nevertheless, HREI had to offer temporary concessions to new tenants in Denver. Leasing in the office buildings in Houston and Charlotte was also "soft."

On June 1, 1983, a $35 million stock issue, the Trust's first since its IPO in 1969, gave HREI the means to continue to grow in this new direction. The Trust's dividend reinvestment plan was also helping to fuel its favorable cash position, producing about $1.75 million a year of new equity by 1984. By the fall of 1983, between cash and equivalents, HREI would have about $50 million to invest.

It seemed in the early 1980s that the REIT was always going "shopping," and prominent on the shopping list were those office buildings. In September 1983, the trustees agreed to buy the Giffels Office Building in Southfield, Michigan. HREI acquired the property at the beginning of 1984 in partnership with a local developer and would hold it throughout vast changes in the REIT, disposing of it in 2005. Giffels Associates, the main tenant, was an engineering and architecture firm.

In March 1984, the advisor recommended a partnership to build a high-tech building in Marlborough, Massachusetts. Although authorized by the trustees, the acquisition fell through. Murdoch later recalled that in stressing diversification through its office building ventures and shopping center purchases, HREI was responding not only to the conventional wisdom accepted by business leaders at the time, but also to what shareholders and potential shareholders wanted to see. For the first time, in 1983, the Trust's annual report categorized its holdings under the headings of "retail," "office," and "distribution and service." According to Murdoch, "Our investors wanted all the diversity they could get."

Wanting diversity and fulfilling that wish with appropriate properties that represented real value for the Trust was not always an easy task. "You can't wait for ten years to find a perfect so-and-so because you have money and you have to invest that money," Trustee Jim York remembered of the early 1980s. "You're looking for a combination of properties with money you have available to put to work." But "the combination of the qualities of the properties you want and the properties actually available doesn't match at any given time."

Hubbard's steady performance in these years was especially impressive in the light of economic conditions that the Trust described in its annual report as "particularly unsettled." A recession in 1982 slowed HREI's investment program momentarily and made leasing at its new office buildings more difficult than it might otherwise have been. The next few years brought somewhat better conditions, with the lower inflation and declining interest rates brought about by President Reagan's economic policies. Fixed rate, long-term financing, however, remained hard to come by. Nevertheless, as a long-run proposition, investing in office buildings would always be a cyclical proposition. And the substantial amounts of capital they required made it often more necessary to own them in partnership with others, thus diluting the REIT's control over its property.

Anyone investing in large office buildings had better be ready to ride a roller coaster: boom and bust was an old story in that sector of the real estate business. In the midst of the expansiveness phase of the cycle, HREI got an early warning of possible contraction. Charles J. Urstadt told his fellow board members in the summer of 1982 that he had inspected its new Denver office property, and while he was pleased with it, he also "commented upon the very large number of office buildings under construction in the Denver area at the present time." The 1982 annual report would reflect the consequences of what Urstadt had observed, commenting on the Denver area that "the supply of space is greater than can be absorbed currently" and that leasing had "slowed considerably" over the past year. "Weak demand" and slow leasing also characterized the Charlotte area. In 1983 the Trust would describe occupancy there as "low." Problems with the local economy in Portland, where HREI now had effective control in its partnership, also threatened to slow leasing there, although up to that point HREI's building in that city was holding its own. Houston, where HREI had its oldest investment in office space, in 1983 had "one of the nation's most overbuilt markets," according to the Trust, which was nevertheless satisfied that leasing had dropped off only "a bit."

Buildings magazine, in its January 1983 issue, quoted Howard L. Ecker, whose real estate firm had compiled a semiannual survey of national office market conditions for each of the previous twelve years: "What we are seeing today is the result of an amount of office space being completed in 1982 that equals completion totals of the previous three years, combined, and is double the aggregate of office building completions for 1977 and 1978." The article went on to cite the views of HREI's William F. Murdoch, who added a note of optimism. He was still seeing leasing activity in his REIT's markets and that indicated "progress." With memories of the terrible real estate recession of the 1970s still fresh in many minds, Murdoch saw no comparison to that debacle. This time around investments were more carefully considered and carried out with a more "professional" attitude. Further, expectations now were more realistic than in the 1970s.

In fact, Murdoch had reason to be optimistic. By the end of fiscal 1984, leasing was up at all HREI office locations. In Southfield, Michigan, where the Giffels Building had been only 60 percent leased when HREI invested in it, the end of 1984 saw it entirely leased up. During that year, the Trust also bought out its partner in Denver, giving it sole ownership of that office building.

Meanwhile, in its retail holdings, which were less subject to the rough ride provided by the office building boom-and-bust phenomenon, the Trust made steady progress. It rightfully boasted to shareholders in 1983 that the retail properties had "performed well." The new leases that gave the REIT a percentage of its tenants' profits were beginning to pay off. Percentage rents in that year produced $480,000, compared to the $48,000 they had brought in five years previously. The continuing success of the retail part of its portfolio would loom large less than a decade later when the Trust would undergo significant changes in its management and its investment goals.

Out with the Old

The property that Hubbard Real Estate Investments sold in the early part of the decade changed the character of HREI's portfolio as much as what it bought. In 1983 it sold thirty-four Safeway stores, at the core of the REITs initial portfolio, back to Safeway for $19.5 million, with payments stretched out over seven years. Each of these stores had a net lease with rents that would have stepped down by more than one-third upon renewal. That same year the Trust also sold the

Carter-Hawley store in Riverside, California, back to that department store firm for $3,852,000; and it sold the Ashland Oil research and office complex in Ohio back to Ashland. Renewal rents there would have dropped by close to a third. These properties were to be the last containing the step-down rents in the renewal clause of their leases other than the Albany, Georgia, Firestone Warehouse where the tenant had an option to buy the property for $1 at lease end.

In little more than a decade, there had been a virtually complete turnover in Hubbard Real Estate Investment's portfolio. Growth had replaced "fixed investment" in both the Trust's philosophy and the nature of the real estate it held. By the end of 1983, which the Trust described as a "watershed year" for HREI, it was no longer burdened by investments that involved no-growth rents. The Trust owned twenty-three commercial properties in fourteen states, including a million square feet of retail space and five office buildings. "We are now generally satisfied with the real estate assets we hold," the Trust contentedly reported to shareholders in its 1983 annual report. Its shareholders, of whom there were now about eight thousand, also had reason to feel contentment. They enjoyed steadily increasing dividends over the next three years, rising from $2.15 a share in 1983 to $2.28 in 1986.

In 1985 the Trust made its largest investment up to that date in any one property, acquiring for $18.5 million a 49 percent stake in the 225,000-square-foot Countryside Village Shopping Center in Clearwater, Florida, from the developer who built it.

Also during that year, the Trust added 70,000 square feet to its Springfield, Massachusetts, shopping center to bring it up to a total of 277,000 square feet. Channel Home Centers, an anchor tenant, leased 50,000 square feet.

HREI in 1985 also acquired a 50 percent interest, with partner Santa Anita Realty Enterprises, Inc., a West Coast REIT, in Civic Center Plaza Towers in Santa Anita, California. The Trust invested $18 million in the eleven-story, 167,000-square-feet office building.

The minutes of a November 1984 trustee's meeting reflect the consensus that "in a market of potential interest rate declines, participating mortgages were viewed as an attractive hedge." At the next meeting, on November 9, the board approved such an investment in a sixty-one-thousand-square-foot suburban office building in DeWitt, New York, near Syracuse. In 1985, HREI funded a $5 million participating mortgage in the building.

Disposing of the "Advisor"

If diversity were truly a measure of success, then the variety of properties HREI owned, the more complex and profitable leases it was negotiating, and the geographical spread of the various locations where it owned or was seeking to buy properties marked the REIT as a success.

As the Trust and at least some of its trustees began to function more as a traditional real estate business, seeking to maximize the bottom line and shareholder value by controlling operating costs while buying and selling properties and leasing them at the firm's maximum advantage, it found itself straining against the very business model built by law into the structure of every REIT. Under most circumstances, it still couldn't directly manage its own property. It was saddled with its advisor—and the advisor's fees. And its advisor's staff and management were serving more than one master.

The Trust's relationship to its advisor was, among other things, financial. A prime motivation for large companies to set up a REIT had been, as noted earlier, the fees they might reap from the REIT's activities. Every year the trustees of the Hubbard Real Estate Investment Trust had to decide whether the REIT would accommodate the advisor's perennial requests for increased fees for its work. The 1980 deliberation, as reflected in the minutes of the board's meeting on September 23, was typical, with some disquiet being expressed, but the relationship remaining unchanged: "There was a consensus that the investment approach of the Adviser, emphasizing significant growth in the portfolio and a disposition of a substantial portion of the Trust's fixed income portfolio, with reinvestment in development and properties, was in the Trust's best interests and supported the Adviser's request for additional compensation."

At the beginning of January 1981, the trustees agreed to pay its advisor on the basis of a new cost-plus fee system beginning later in the year. That system was not quite as simple and transparent as it might have seemed at first was shown when the advisor moved to 2 Broadway in New York City's downtown financial district in mid-1981. The advisor's rent would increase. Should that new figure be used as part of the "cost" of its operations in determining its compensation from HREI? Not according to the trustees, who decided to use average occupancy rates to calculate the advisor's operating cost.

Increasingly, conflict of interest was an issue between the Trust and its advisor. This problem was endemic between REITs and their advisors. In the case of Hubbard Real Estate Investments, its problems with Merrill Lynch Hubbard—and by extension, Merrill Lynch, of which the advisor was a subsidiary—worsened until they became virtually intolerable.

By 1979, the trustees discomfort level with Merrill Lynch Hubbard's staff handling other real estate operations besides HREI's had already led it to take action. At their meeting on January 22, 1979, the trustees had insisted on the establishment of a separate subsidiary of Merrill Lynch Hubbard dedicated solely to HREI. It had resulted in the creation of that subsidiary, the Hubbard Advisory Corporation.

As the 1980s began, potential conflicts of interest between the advisor's outside work and loyalties and the services it provided for HREI seemed to become more prominent and problematic. Merrill Lynch Hubbard was becoming part of Merrill Lynch's newly expanded real estate operations, which in 1982 would see the big brokerage house set up Merrill Lynch Realty as a holding company to handle its real estate operations. The advisor owed it to Merrill Lynch to make a profit based on facilitating deals between companies. They owed it to HREI to choose possible acquisitions and dispositions based solely on what was good for HREI and its shareholders. But that set up the potential scenario of the advisor deciding that what would be good for HREI was to buy a property for sale by one of Merrill Lynch's clients, or to sell to one of those clients, which was sometimes the case. For example, at the trustees meeting on May 5, 1979, on the table for discussion, at the suggestion of the advisor, was a proposal by a Richard Spangler to sell warehouses in Charlotte, North Carolina, to HREI. According to the minutes, he "had been referred to the Advisor through Mr. Spangler's acquaintances at Merrill Lynch." Spangler was willing to accept HREI stock as payment for the property, but the trustees decided that the transaction was not a favorable one for the Trust.

Offers from outsiders to buy the Trust, received via the advisor, were made from time to time; and the trustees were bound by their responsibility under the law to consider if any of them might be advantageous to the Trust and its shareholders. For example, at their September 6, 1979, meeting, the advisor had informed the trustees that Wimpey's, a British land company, had expressed some interest in buying the REIT; but nothing further developed. More serious was the possible deal revealed at the meeting of July 30, 1980. A Merrill Lynch representative attended that meeting to discuss the interest expressed to it by the Oregon Public Employee Retirement System to possibly buy HREI. The board agreed to give the offer serious consideration and hired the real estate firm of James Landauer to review the value of the Trust's portfolio with a view to a possible sale. But in early 1981, Landauer was told to halt its work when it became clear that the deal would not go through.

At least one trustee had raised the issue of a possible conflict of interest by Merrill Lynch in acting as the Trust's investment banker in such a deal, as well as serving in a similar role for the prospective purchaser. The trustees considered the problem but, at the time, decided that since HREI was such a small part of the brokerage house's business, a conflict of interest did not exist.

In the fall of 1982, First Union Realty Trust broached to Merrill Lynch the possibility of buying HREI but did not make a specific offer. However, the matter did not die; and at the board of trustees' meeting on January 12, 1983, the plot really thickened. At this meeting, which directly preceded the annual shareholder's meeting, William F. Murdoch, the minutes noted, said that "Dennis Hess, President of Merrill Lynch Realty, Inc., had within the past week recommended to him and requested that he propose to the Trustees that they consider liquidation of the trust. In addition, Mr. Hess had also informed him of the [interest of] the Reliance Insurance Group in purchasing a substantial minority interest in the Trust and of the interest of First Union Realty in the possibility of acquiring the Trust."

Murdoch went on to note that "Merrill Lynch was the investment banker of both parties and that the Merrill Lynch executive who had reported the Reliance Company's interest was a director of one of the Reliance Group Companies."

Further, a lawyer representing the Trust's advisor, Merrill Lynch Hubbard, had communicated to a member of the law firm representing the Trust that the Reliance Group was serious and that that firm "represented a valued client of Merrill Lynch, that Merrill Lynch hoped that any transaction might be friendly and that Merrill Lynch would like to represent the Reliance group in a deal with the trust."

The minutes of the trustees next meeting, on March 8, 1983, report: "There was general concern at what appeared to be the initiation by one or more representatives of Merrill Lynch of contacts with Merrill Lynch customers regarding possible tenders or efforts to acquire the Trust or a significant interest in the Trust without prior consultation with or authorization by the Trustees." The dry language that recounts this reaction belies the emotion in the room. Charles J. Urstadt, for one, was very unhappy. He thought that this was outrageous behavior by at least a few individuals at Merrill Lynch involving a clear conflict of interest and it was going to stop if he could do anything about it.

The minutes went on to record the trustees' agreement that "Mr. Urstadt would contact Goldman Sachs about the possibility of their providing the Trust with investment bank services." Urstadt knew that the firm had a strong reputation for helping to defend against takeovers. He called an old acquaintance, John Whitehead at Goldman Sachs, who agreed to provide that service. The trustees also decided that the independent trustees—those with no connections to Merrill Lynch and its advisor—would meet with Merrill Lynch executives to discuss the situation and "clarify Merrill Lynch's position with respect to the trust and the determination of the Trustees to maintain the independence of the trust at this time. Merrill Lynch would also be informed of the disposition of the Trustees to internalize the advisory function." This was as close as the trustees could come at the time to a virtual declaration of independence from its sponsor and the advisor the sponsor had provided to guide the Trust.

In a crucial meeting, Urstadt presented the REIT's position to then Merrill executive Donald Regan. The upshot was that Merrill Lynch backed off.

In fact, for some time, the trustees had been signaling their frustration with having to leave everything but their final approval or disapproval to the advisor. The board had taken a step toward a more active role at its meeting of September 6, 1979, when it created a Project Review Committee, which included Urstadt among its members, to supervise additions to the HREI portfolio already approved by the board. Murdoch would question even the sufficiency of that step a year later when he suggested to the board that they needed a more powerful body. The minutes of the August 6, 1980, meeting report that the Trust's president "noted the need for quick reaction in order to conclude negotiations in the real estate field and the difficulty which the trust from time to time had had in reacting quickly enough to maximize an investment opportunity."

In September 1984, Murdoch suggested that HREI hire an employment consulting firm to assess its executive incentive compensation program, but the trustees rebuffed him, preferring to handle the task internally. They renamed the Trust's Stock Options Committee the Executive Compensation and Stock Option Committee. Two months later, the trustees made more explicit their desire that HREI manage its own affairs. They directed Murdoch to examine the possibility of restructuring the Trust's relationship to its advisor. In December, the trustees set up a committee to meet with Merrill Lynch Hubbard, "with a view to concluding an arrangement which would provide the trust with greater flexibility and control over key personnel."

At this point the battle for the Trust's independence was moving beyond the boardroom to the halls of Congress. As has been pointed out in chapter 1, sentiment had been growing throughout the REIT industry to restructure that part of the federal tax code governing real estate investment trusts to allow them to manage their own affairs. "Self-management" was the word of the day. At their March 12, 1985, meeting, the trustees authorized a $1,000 contribution to NAREIT's campaign to accomplish just that.

Independence Day

In a classic bit of understatement, Murdoch began his message to shareholders in the 1985 annual report with, "The year 1985 was one of the most important in our history."

The 1986 change in the federal tax code would produce multiple fundamental changes in Hubbard Real Estate Investments. The business possibilities these changes created would ultimately lead to new management, a new business plan, a new location, and even a new name. In fact, within a few short years, the real estate investment trust business would be almost unrecognizable.

In his report to shareholders assessing the effect of the change in the tax code after it took effect, Murdoch would write, "The basic REIT concept is unchanged, but now we have more flexibility. We can manage some properties directly without an independent manager; we can sell more properties in one year under a 'safe harbor' provision; and we can limit our liability through subsidiary corporations."

The reference to that "independent manager" was a telling one. Before it could create something new, the Trust had to break something old: its ties to its advisor. On December 17, 1985, empowered by the coming change in the tax code, the board of trustees of the Hubbard Real Estate Investment Trust voted the following: "Resolved: That the Advisory Agreement between Hubbard Real Estate Investments and Merrill Lynch Hubbard shall be allowed to terminate effective January 31, 1986." At that same meeting, the trustees changed the name of the Trust to HRE Properties and voted to move its headquarters from 2 Broadway, to which it had moved from Massachusetts only a year earlier to be near its Merrill Lynch Hubbard advisor, to 530 Fifth Avenue, a location unrelated to Merrill Lynch. The name HRE, incidentally, was a matter of convenience: It meant that the Trust could continue to use the same symbol it had been using on the New York Stock Exchange.

The *Wall Street Journal* reported the change on December 20, 1985, noting that the new name would take effect on February 1, 1986. "Personnel now employed by the adviser will move to the trust," the paper stated. "Hubbard says it doesn't expect any change in its business operations."

Expectations notwithstanding, the Trust's business operations would soon take a new turn. More immediately, control of HRE Properties was about to take a dramatic turn, and the cast of characters who would play in that drama had also been going through some changes. The old guard that had created the Trust was passing from the scene. John Hubbard died in 1986. George "Morry" Hubbard had retired from the advisor at the end of 1974, but had remained on the board of trustees until 1984, when he became a trustee emeritus. Brinley M. Hall, who had been serving as the equivalent of the Trust's CFO virtually since its inception, announced his retirement in 1984 and was replaced by Harold Salm in 1985. Salm, in turn, would be replaced by Stephen C. Hagen, who became the REIT's treasurer the same year. Architect Bryant Young had joined the advisor in 1985 and almost immediately went to work directing the expansion of the Springfield Shopping Center and the redevelopment of the Newington, New Hampshire, property from a warehouse facility to a mixed-use development. Paul Paganucci, chairman of the Executive Committee and director of W. R. Grace & Co. and a financial vice president of Dartmouth College and former associate dean of the Tuck School of Business Administration at Dartmouth, was added to the board of directors in November 1984.

In 1987, James R. Moore would join HRE—and remain with the company, eventually becoming its CFO, through its transformation into Urstadt Biddle Properties. Moore, a CPA, had been a senior manager at Ernst & Young. He had extensive experience in all the financial aspects of real estate, including matters related to regional shopping centers, expertise that would serve him well in the near future.

Outwardly, one might observe little that had changed since the Trust had become independent, at least initially. HRE inherited HREI's portfolio and its people. The employees of the advisor, Merrill Lynch Hubbard, who had been working on the Trust's investment program, were now working directly for HRE; and in September 1986, HRE set up a profit-sharing and savings plan for them. Murdoch was still president of the Trust, answerable to the board of trustees.

More change was in the air. At the trustees meeting on December 16, 1986, according to the minutes of that meeting, "Mr. Paganucci reflected on the need for the President to be able to work on the substantive items to be presented at the Trustee meetings. It was suggested by Mr. Paganucci that a board chairman could assist the President with his more general duties (i.e. presiding over meeting [sic], discussing possible agenda issues with the Trustees, etc.) Mr. Paganucci then recommended Mr. Urstadt for the new position of Chairman of the Board of HRE Properties." The election to the unpaid position was unanimous. It was in fact the first step toward a change in control of the Trust, a change that would also bring with it a change in the direction in which the Trust had been moving.

This change in control would occur under fire. The event that would precipitate the changeover was a hostile takeover attempt by Kimco, a large and formidable Long Island shopping center owner.

Kimco

In the mid-1980s, mergers and acquisitions and takeover attempts, hostile and friendly, filled the financial pages. The minutes of the HREI's board of trustees meetings tell us that as early as March 12, 1985, the trustees met with HREI's legal counsel "to discuss the various measures which might be available to deal with attempts to obtain control of the Trust."

Perhaps the Trust was already girding for a struggle over its existence when it decided to devote the 1986 annual report to a group portrait of its trustees. Each was portrayed on half a page with a black-and-white photo over a brief biography. It was as if they were saying to shareholders, "You know who we are, our backgrounds are a matter of public record, and you can trust us." The alternative was to take the word of unfamiliar outsiders that they could do a better job of wringing profits from HRE.

Control of the Trust could pass to new hands without outside intervention. An individual or group of insiders could buy enough shares to exert control. At the trustees meeting on September 18, 1987, Urstadt and Martin Cleary informed the board that they were filing the required SEC documents declaring that they had accumulated "more than 5% of the outstanding common shares of HRE." By March 1988, Urstadt had purchased twenty-four thousand additional shares.

At the board of trustees meeting on June 14, the trustees were officially informed that Urstadt has purchased Martin Cleary's shares.

But Urstadt and Cleary were not the only ones in the running for control of the Trust at this time. Milton Cooper, head of Kimco Development Corporation had also set his sights on acquiring HRE Properties and had informed Murdoch and Urstadt of his intentions. Now the trustees learned that Kimco had filed SEC Schedule 14D, formally announcing its intentions. Founded in 1958 by Cooper and Martin Kimmel when they invested in a Florida shopping center, and incorporated in 1966, Kimco was a substantial force to be reckoned with.

Urstadt's clear bid to become a direct force in HRE was by no means a sure thing. To prevent any hostile takeovers, there was a provision in the Trust's rules and regulations that allowed it to redeem the holdings of any group or individual whose ownership exceeded 9.9 percent of all shares outstanding, which now applied to Urstadt's holdings. Cooper had demanded that the trustees invoke this provision and redeem Urstadt's shares. At the September 18 meeting, Urstadt was asked to leave the room so the other trustees could decide whether or not to redeem his shares. They declined to redeem the Urstadt shares.

On August 22, 1988, the *Wall Street Journal* reported that Kimco headed a group that had already acquired 5.3 percent of HRE's shares "and might seek a greater role in the New York real estate investment trust." Kimco had filed with the SEC its intentions to discuss with the Trust's present management how HRE's bottom line could be improved by new ownership, a move that signaled Kimco's intention to apply a "bear hug" to HRE. The story also reported that "a New York company controlled by Charles J. Urstadt, chairman of HRE's Board of Trustees, boosted its stake in HRE to 12.6% of the concern's shares. The company, Pearce, Urstadt, Mayer & Greer Inc., said it bought 179,600 shares [Martin Cleary's stake] on Aug. 10 from three officers of Jacobs, Visconsi & Jacobs, a Cleveland real estate development firm."

HRE Properties' trustees were now in the middle of a battle between two men determined to control the Trust. Legal counsel was present to advise the trustees on their obligations to shareholders in the contest for the Trust. They were obliged to act "in good faith," they were told, keeping in mind both the interests of the business and those of the shareholders. That didn't necessarily mean just digging in their heels to retain present management come hell or high water. On the other hand, the minutes recount, "defensive actions taken against takeovers or takeover tactics are not improper." The deciding factor was the "business judgment" rule, which was "a presumption that in making a business decision the directors of a corporation acted on an informed basis, in good faith and in the honest belief that the actions they took were in the best interests of the corporation."

If there were any doubts about which way the trustees were leaning after they declined to redeem Urstadt's shares, there could be none when later in the meeting they replaced Martin Cleary, who had resigned as a trustee, with George H. C. Lawrence, a director of the Urstadt Property Company, the private firm through which Charles J. Urstadt controlled his personal real estate holdings. Lawrence was also CEO of Lawrence Investing Company of Bronxville, New York.

By the meeting of October 27, 1988, the HRE Properties Board of Trustees was on a war footing. At that meeting, their counsel went over various strategies they might use to thwart Kimco, including an unlimited stock authorization and a requirement that new trustees be nominated in advance by shareholders. They also considered the possibilities of incorporating in various states with laws that would help them in their efforts to fend off their huge and unfriendly suitor from Roslyn, Long Island. Merrill Lynch, which the trustees had engaged to advise them on practical measures they could take, proposed a Series A Participating Preferred Shares program. The trustees adopted the idea and authorized 150,000 shares. If Kimco tried to swallow up HRE, it would have to down a "poison pill" with it. The trustees also adopted a resolution that any nomination for a new trustee would have to be submitted at least sixty days before the next shareholders meeting.

The shareholder rights plan that came out of this meeting involving the preferred shares was "complex," as the Trust itself described it. The one paragraph reference to it in the 1988 annual report referred shareholders to a footnote in the midst of the financial performance section of the report for a more detailed explanation. In the note to shareholders in the front of the report, the Trust stated: "The Plan is intended to protect shareholder interests in the event the Trust is confronted with coercive or unfair takeover tactics." That was the only reference in the report to the struggle that had begun with Kimco.

On November 23, there were "golden parachutes" in the air as the Trust's Compensation Committee met to discuss stock options and their relation to "change of control" of the company. They talked about measures "which would trigger the right to walk if the office of the trust were moved outside Manhattan rather than outside New York City, as presently provided." These measures were installed in the Trust's rules and regulations. They also raised the issue of possibly accelerated deferred payments if control changed.

Much of the action now went on behind the scenes, with the combatants unofficially communicating with each other as they jockeyed for position. At the December 13, 1988, meeting, the minutes record a cryptic exchange: "Mr. Murdoch described a recent conversation he had with Mr. Cooper. The Trustees discussed Mr. Cooper's comments." This terse, tantalizing entry provides no further specifics.

Three weeks later, on January 5, 1989, the board of trustees added to its members E. Virgil Conway, CEO of the Seaman's Bank for Savings in New York, another Urstadt ally. Urstadt had also added another 26,800 shares of HRE to his holdings, and again he was asked to step outside while the board decided not to exercise its option to redeem them. The trustees also reviewed a letter from Kimco, but its contents are not described in the minutes.

The trustees still had a conflict of interest problem with Merrill Lynch. This time HRE needed an investment banker to represent it in its struggle with Kimco, and representatives of Merrill Lynch Capital Markets were at this meeting to argue their case to be the one chosen. HRE president Murdoch, however, threw cold water on their chances when he described to the trustees "a relationship which had developed between Merrill Lynch and Kimco." The minutes tell us merely that the trustees were concerned with that relationship "and Merrill Lynch's representation of the Trust in the current context."

When the trustees met on March 28 to choose an investment banker from among Merrill Lynch, Goldman Sachs, and First Boston Corporation, it was almost a foregone conclusion that Merrill Lynch would be the first to be eliminated. Merrill Lynch offered to secure from Kimco an assurance that it would have no objection to Merrill Lynch representing HRE, but it was not Kimco's possible objection that concerned the HRE trustees. Their own objection to Merrill Lynch's playing both sides at once was more to the point. "After discussion," relate the minutes, "the Trustees concluded that Merrill Lynch's conflict of interest effectively precluded them from representation of the trust." Goldman Sachs was approved because its terms "were more favorable to the trust."

In an April 6 letter agreement, HRE agreed to pay Goldman Sachs $150,000 per quarter plus expenses to serve as its investment banker in the ongoing battle with Kimco. That "expenses" part is more than just a formality. The agreement specified that expenses could include "legal counsel, surveyors, engineers and other professionals," indicating that once the meter started to run, the expenses were potentially substantial. Should HRE decide to sell to Kimco, Goldman's cut would range anywhere from 5/8 percent "of the aggregate consideration" to as much as 1 1/4 percent, depending on the kind of deal that was struck. As a coda to the agreement with Goldman Sachs, the board meeting minutes for April 7 note: "Mr. Murdoch stated that he had a conversation with Merrill Lynch and had informed them that their services to the Trust were being terminated."

Just over three weeks later, the trustees took up a complaint from their own president that employees of the Trust, from the lowest to the highest, were still not receiving adequate protection in the event of a sale. Murdoch "had indicated concern that the existing arrangements were insufficient for retention purposes and that there were staff perceptions that the existing arrangements offered inadequate protection in the event of a change of control." Specifically, Murdoch was worried that a new owner could cut the lines of the golden parachutes written into the Trust's rules and regulations by dismissing for "cause." To satisfy this anxiety, the trustees tightened the definition of "cause" to mean only major infractions such as dishonesty or conflict of interest, and they established levels of severance pay for the four secretaries who worked for HRE.

By March 1989, HRE had a formal offer from the Kimco Development Corporation for $27 a share for those shares Kimco didn't already own, an offer which would come to slightly more than $148 million. Kimco valued HRE at $160 million, according to *The New York Times*. The news that HRE might be in play sent its stock up $3.37 to $25. That gain of more than 15 percent was the second largest that day on the New York Stock Exchange. Of the six million shares of HRE outstanding, Kimco had reported acquiring 8.6 percent.

The trustees met on May 7 to consider the offer. Present to advise them were counsel from two firms: Ropes & Gray and Shearman & Sterling. Having valued the Trust at between $28.15 and $31.65 a share, Goldman Sachs "was of the opinion that the $27 per share price in the Kimco proposal was inadequate." The trustees added to the expert opinion their own sense of the Trust's valuation, the market condition, etc. and, keeping in mind the "business judgment" rule so carefully explained to them by counsel at a meeting almost two years previously, found that "there was unanimous agreement that the Kimco proposal was inadequate and that it was not in the best interests of the Trust to seek any sale of the trust at this time."

In July Kimco hired Wertheim Schroder & Company to advise it in its attempt to take over HRE Properties, and in September, Kimco signaled a proxy fight when it demanded a list of HRE shareholders. Kimco aimed for a special shareholders meeting to oust the current trustees, replacing them with trustees "committed to realizing the underlying value of the trust's properties."

Next came a move that changed the history of HRE. At their meeting on September 19, 1989, the board of trustees of HRE Properties acknowledged the facts on the ground. Mr. Urstadt had already secured effective financial control of the Trust, and now he received operating control as well. Murdoch and Urstadt were asked to leave the room while the trustees made the move that would ultimately take the company from a legacy organization of Hubbard Real Estate Investments to the direct precursor of Urstadt Biddle Properties. They discussed "Mr. Urstadt's position as Chairman and largest beneficial stockholder of the Trust and his proposed election as President and Chief Executive Officer of the Trust to serve without compensation." The vote to put Urstadt at the head of HRE was at this point a formality and quickly done. They also "agreed to accept Mr. Murdoch's resignation as President of the Trust." As consolation, Murdoch was made vice chairman, receiving a new employment and consultant contract. Stephen Hagen was named executive vice president, and James Moore became a senior vice president.

The board of trustees ultimately responsible for running HRE now had seven members: George T. Conklin, Jr.; E. Virgil Conway; George H. C. Lawrence;

William F. Murdoch, Jr.; Paul D. Paganucci; Charles J. Urstadt; and James O. York. Only Conklin was a holdover from the original group that had first guided HREI, and only he and Murdoch represented the Hubbard influence.

Kimco and its quest to absorb HRE were by now on the agenda at every board meeting. At the meeting on November 14, it was noted that Kimco had backed off on its demand for a special shareholders meeting. But Kimco was making its mark on HRE even short of taking it over. According to the minutes, "Mr. Moore noted that Trust operations in the fourth quarter continued to show slight improvement but that all of the improvement was offset by the costs of the Kimco matter." Kimco and its maneuverings were a drain on the Trust's resources and cut into the time that the Trust's officers and employees would have been better spending on improving HRE's business prospects.

Stockholders and the general public had been given some of the bare facts of the Kimco attempt at a hostile takeover in the financial press. In HRE's 1989 annual report, the Trust berated Kimco while discussing its "financial results," stating that HRE had done reasonably well despite expenses incurred in fighting off the Roslyn, Long Island, firm. HRE summarized the Kimco story up to that point in three paragraphs in the middle of the "To Our Shareholders" section under the heading, "Kimco Matters." Then the Trust stated: "The Trustees are always open to genuine proposals that are truly beneficial to all shareholders, but Kimco's actions this year have been no more than harassment. They have hurt all shareholders by diverting management time from our business, and have caused us to spend substantial amounts of our shareholders money."

There followed a section called "Management," containing a single paragraph noting the change in leadership at HRE. On that page was a color portrait of HRE's new CEO, Charles J. Urstadt.

The struggle against the threat from outside continued into 1990. In January 1990, Kimco amended the SEC Schedule 13D that it had filed only a few weeks before, on December 11, 1989, which had stated that Kimco owned 601,050 shares of HRE. Now they acknowledged that, for some time, two other groups allied with them, Delafield Asset Management and Shufro, Rose & Ehrman had also been acquiring shares—283,300 and 305,450 shares respectively. The trustees voted to redeem these shares at a cost of $13.5 million.

On March 22, 1990, the trustees assessed the effect of the Kimco battle on HRE's financial position. The struggle had reduced the then-current cash flow to $0.25 a share compared to $0.42 in the same period in the previous year. The consequence was inevitable: the board had to cut the quarterly dividend to $0.25 a share. By May, the battle had also taken its toll on HRE's share price, which had declined to 16 5/8.

Only in hindsight do we know that this was about the worst of it. By June, cash flow was back to $0.46 a share and HRE was able to increase the quarterly dividend to a satisfactory $0.45 a share. Over the course of 1990, the need to fend off Kimco would cost HRE about $0.17 a share. But in its 1990 annual report, HRE did not even feel the necessity of any longer mentioning Kimco in its note "To Our Shareholders."

In mid-1991, the Trust discovered that Kimco's allies were still buying HRE shares and demanded that these members of the Kimco group comply with SEC rules and promptly disclose any such purchases. The board countered the purchases by redeeming fifty-two thousand of the shares they had bought.

And slowly, without the drama of the battle at its height, the attempt by Kimco Development to stage a hostile takeover of HRE Properties faded. David had not slain Goliath, but had won simply by surviving in its present form, free to develop its business as it saw fit. And amidst the clamor of battle, that development had already taken some new, interesting, and ultimately productive and profitable turns.

Chapter Four

A NEW BUSINESS PLAN

The elevation of Charles J. Urstadt to CEO of HRE Properties in 1989 was occasioned by the fight to keep the company from being swallowed up by Kimco. But the ultimate significance of the move went far beyond HRE's prolonged struggle to remain independent. In fact, the consequences of Urstadt's new position for HRE's ongoing operations would completely overshadow Kimco's attempt at a hostile takeover.

Urstadt did not just represent a new face at the top of HRE. He was not at the helm just to guide it through the current storm. He was a man with a plan and stood for an entirely new direction in the company's business. Indeed, at their meeting of September 19, 1989, the trustees not only voted to make Urstadt HRE's CEO, they also voted acceptance of his business plan to redirect the Trust, geographically consolidating its holdings in the Northeast while focusing on the acquisition and management of neighborhood shopping centers.

Urstadt dedicated himself to fending off Kimco because, first of all, he firmly believed that HRE could maximize its profits by staying small. For Urstadt, it was a matter of basic business philosophy. "In large companies, entrepreneurial decisions do not exist," Urstadt, who had learned from experience, said. "Only the political perspective does. People try to impress the boss as they seek various perks." Having served at or near the top in several major real estate firms, as the head of New York State's Division of Housing and Community Renewal and as the first chairman and chief executive officer of the Battery Park City Authority where he had to deal with government bureaucracy at the city, state, and federal levels, Urstadt knew what large organizations entailed. Size mattered, and he wanted to keep HRE small, flexible, and responsive.

Related to size was distance—the geographical distance from a real estate company to the properties it owned and managed. Shrink the distance and you achieve greater efficiency and, with it, lower operating and managerial costs. Urstadt couldn't abide the Trust's scattershot approach to property location and the lack of real estate business savvy that attitude reflected. Years later, he would criticize the boards' simplistic concept that had them putting "two charts in each report: one was a chart of the United States and the other was a chart of the diversity of its property types. It seemed like the board was trying to color in all the states."

Urstadt's grandfather, who had influenced him to go into real estate, had told him, "You ought to be able to walk to what you owned." In this day and age, that was no longer always practical. But management should still be able to reach their company's properties with no more than an hour or two behind the wheel, Urstadt believed. Ultimately that would be refined to a geographical criterion for HRE acquisitions that confined most of the Trust's new investment possibilities to within about a 50-75 mile radius of corporate headquarters, a standard for acquisitions that remains in effect today at Urstadt Biddle Properties.

As with geography, so with diversity. Scattering HRE's property over multiple types of real estate investment was not likely to produce the best result. Concentrating on one sector in the business, ideally one more insulated from the inevitable boom-and-bust cycles that affected office buildings, was a better bet. The investment also ought to be in something that best matched the experience and skills of HRE's personnel. Retail properties had good long-term prospects in the late 1980s, and there were already people on board at the Trust who had experience in that area. Concentrating on the ownership of such properties would further hone the skills of HRE personnel, paying handsome dividends in lower management and operational costs.

Furthermore, the market recently seemed to be saying that HRE, and HREI before it, had gone too far along the road to diversity. All the signs pointed in one direction. As Trustee Jim York later recalled of that turning point in the company's history, CEO Urstadt was determined to "undiversify." His approach was to put most of the company's eggs in one basket and then watch the basket.

What should go into that basket? Neighborhood shopping centers, especially ones anchored by supermarkets and featuring such basics as drug stores and personal service businesses such as barbershops, were more likely to negotiate the ups and downs of the economy and still remain upright. Even in hard times, people had to eat and get their hair cut. So it would be back to meat-and-potatoes basics in its most literal sense.

If the Trust chose well among potential shopping center acquisitions and effectively managed what it chose, adding value by making attractive and practical renovations, securing the right mix of tenants, and negotiating the best possible leases with them, HRE could go on paying steady dividends while generating capital appreciation. Ultimately that's what it was all about. The Trust hadn't missed a dividend yet since its formation in 1969, and there wasn't going to be a first time on Charles J. Urstadt's watch.

Urstadt was clearly going to put his imprint on HRE Properties, but it wasn't going to be a one-man show. Far from it. Urstadt was of the old school that said you bring in the best people and then let them do what you hired them to do. Early on, he set out the criteria for choosing Trust personnel, and they remain the same today:

1. You have to be grounded with an education in business and law and economics.
2. You have to be raised in a real estate atmosphere.
3. You have to stay in the business and follow it as a career.
4. You have to know more than anyone else.

"We seek intelligence among our workers," Urstadt said. "With ambition comes competitiveness. You move from one goal to another. You set a goal and you achieve it and then you set another goal. Some people if they lose they give up. What we teach is that success has many fathers." When asked about his operational philosophy, Urstadt was even more succinct, condensing it into the four "go-gets": "Go get the money. Go get the property. Go get the tenants. Go get the rent."

There was one other characteristic of potential Trust personnel that was vitally important to Charles J. Urstadt: he wanted them to want to "own" their work in more than just a metaphorical sense. Urstadt wanted everyone connected to the Trust to act as if he or she had a personal stake in its success because, in fact, they actually did. His main complaint about the old guard among the trustees and management was that they "did not have their own skin in the game." They didn't "have their own savings and their own equity" tied to a healthy bottom line. "It's the difference between owning your own car and renting a car." Self-interest was always the best motivator. The best way to get Trust personnel to care just as much about HRE's financial success as did its shareholders was for them to be shareholders, with holdings as large as possible. Consequently, employee and trustee stock ownership plans would always be a significant part of this REIT under Urstadt's management. In January 1991, HRE began to implement this policy, increasing the potential shares in its stock option plan from 300,000 to 450,000, and adding an annual grant of one thousand shares to nonemployee trustees.

Urstadt also anticipated by many years the more recent criticisms in the financial press about possible conflicts of interest between the exercising of managerial stock options and the conduct of a company's business. He took pains to see to it that the Trust was always managed so as to increase shareholder value and genuine company profitability, not just to produce gaudy numbers from quarter to quarter that temporarily inflated the price of shares, provoking stock analysts to run to their crystal balls and ultimately benefiting mostly insiders holding stock options.

Then there was the matter of the Trust's dividend policy. Setting it higher than was reasonable might temporarily increase the value of the stock, making shareholders happy, at least for a while. But was that a good business decision? The real estate business is an ongoing enterprise, not a short-run contest to see how good one can look from quarter to quarter. Urstadt's idea was to build the business along sound lines, not to drain it of needed resources for short-term payouts when those resources were needed to invest in new properties and upgrade old ones to spur their future growth.

At the trustees meeting on September 19, 1990, Urstadt created the guidelines that HRE would henceforth use to set the quarterly dividend. He told the board that for the first three quarters of that fiscal year, the $1.15 in dividends that had been paid out had "exceeded funds from operations by about $.10 a share." HRE's CEO felt that the issue was important enough to the shareholders to spell out in a press release: "Today's difficult real estate market and uncertain outlook for the economy make it prudent that we provide for contingencies and for future growth. Beginning in fiscal 1991, the Trustees expect to declare dividends at levels not exceeding the Trust's funds from operations taking into account historic and expected fiscal results. HRE believes funds from operations to be the most significant indicator of the trust's performance."

The new HRE was anxious to communicate to its shareholders that this was no longer the staid and static real estate investment trust that Merrill Lynch had created in 1969. What better way to do that than through the pages of its annual report? Any company's annual report is a statement, often made with powerful, persuasive images, about what it is, how it sees itself, and where it aims to go. In several of the HREI reports, the only photographs were of the trustees, a group of well-dressed, predominantly late middle-aged, prosperous-looking gentlemen who could easily have been Wall Street bond traders. The message conveyed through these images was: "We know what we're doing and your money is in good hands. We're going to do this year just what we did last year. Don't worry, there's nothing new under the sun." And the text and financial data presented enhanced that picture.

The 1989 annual report was the first under HRE's new management. In every way it announced a new period in the Trust's history. In his message "To Our Shareholders," Urstadt said:

> The Year 1989 was marked by a major shift in strategy for HRE Properties.
>
> The Trustees and management, after consideration of all available options, concluded that the competitive environment in the real estate

industry dictated a transition from a Trust with properties dispersed nationally to one with its investments concentrated in the eastern part of the United States—where market knowledge, proximity and management experience could be focused in a way that would maximize long-term shareholder value . . . .

Going forward, our plan is to sell approximately $20 million of Trust properties over the next two or three years. The program will be carried out on a highly selective basis with the dual objectives of diminishing the geographic diversity of our portfolio and concentrating our investments and management expertise on properties that meet our criteria for future growth and maximum cash flow. As a result, we expect that future acquisitions will be located in the East.

We also announced in December that we would repurchase periodically up to one million shares of the Trust. We expect to use the proceeds from future property sales as well as available cash to finance the share repurchase program. However, as an interim measure, we may also draw upon a 30-month $25 million term loan facility for which the Trust has a commitment from a commercial bank.

Urstadt concluded his message to shareholders in a direct and personal way that embodied the new attitude to be found at HRE Properties: "My personal commitment to the Trust as the owner of 13% of the outstanding shares indicates my confidence that its values are sound and that I am committed to creating the highest possible future values for all shareholders." And in the 1991 annual report, Urstadt's message to shareholders began not with "To Our Shareholders" but with "Dear Fellow Shareholders." It concluded: "My personal commitment to HRE is unwavering. I own 855,800 shares, or more than 16% of the total, and this includes 25,000 shares I purchased this month."

This 1990 annual report featured photographs of HRE's management in shirtsleeves, conducting meetings, conferring individually with other employees and, generally, hard at work. The visual message was: "We're on the go and getting it done. We're not afraid to make changes, although we will always do so cautiously and prudently."

As an advertising copywriter might have put it: "This is not the REIT your father bought into twenty years ago."

But all of the new plans and new attitudes would have been no more than empty rhetoric, mere public relations, were they not to be effectively implemented and embedded in the day-to-day operation of the Trust. The history of HRE and Urstadt Biddle Properties over the next decade and a half would prove that these words and intentions were not empty but rather a substantive declaration of the way things were going to be from then on.

Back to Business

The thwarted Kimco takeover and the change in management were dramatic highlights of HRE's history in the late 1980s and early 1990s, but there was still a business to run, now that management was actually able to run it directly. If the company were to be made over, it would come about not from dramatic restatements of company philosophy and new faces in company management, but rather from accretions of small and large business decisions, new acquisitions, and the sale of properties that no longer fit into the Trust's new business plan. All of this would be affected and often limited by business conditions, the general state of the economy, and government rules and regulations. This change would not come from someone just snapping his fingers.

For example, the minutes of the trustees meeting for July 18, 1989, indicate sentiment for selling the HRE office buildings in Houston and Portland. That would have begun to change HRE's portfolio dramatically, but the Trust did not want to sell these buildings in a buyer's market, taking a financial hit when that could be avoided by more carefully choosing a time to dispose of them. This was not the right time, and the matter was put off until the market would turn.

The pace of business had slowed while control of the company was in doubt. The REIT that Urstadt assumed control of in the late 1980s was in the doldrums compared to its performance earlier in the decade. Already in 1986, HRE's annual report led off with, "This past year was a difficult one for the real estate industry, and many markets will be no better in 1987. Rental markets were weak on a broad basis, and falling interest rates reduced earnings on our invested cash." FFO was flat and net income off. The 1987 report spoke of "a disappointing year" because leasing was tough in the overbuilt office market sector, leaving HRE with a 12 percent office space vacancy rate. Keeping HRE's buildings competitive drove up expenses, and lower interest rates predominated just as HRE's high-yielding, short-term investments were maturing. Nor did the stock market crash in October 1987 help anyone's bottom line. FFO and net income had taken a hit, and the dividend had declined.

Despite some progress in leasing in 1988, the year that Urstadt began to take control of the Trust, HRE characterized it as "a difficult year for much of the real estate industry and a disappointing one for HRE Properties." Again, overbuilding and inflation were the culprits. "Successful leasing programs raised our occupancy levels but could not offset lower rents and higher costs," HRE informed its shareholders. Cash flow, net income, and dividends were all down. In its April issue that year, *Changing Times*, the Kiplinger publication, expressed skepticism about HRE's short-term prospects, given its slippage in net income, reduced dividend, and declining stock price. Fortunately, the Trust was in business for the long run.

In 1989, while HRE struggled with Kimco, there wasn't too much difference in its operating environment. "In a very difficult year for the real estate industry, HRE Properties performed respectably" was the Trust's middling assessment of its fortunes. Net income increased a whopping 48 percent, but that could be attributed largely to gains from the sale of property. FFO was down.

On the bright side, and more important for its long-run prospects, HRE was beginning to put a tight lid on operating costs. There were efficiencies that could be achieved everywhere, management discovered, even in the way the Trust kept its books. For example, at a meeting of the trustee's Audit Committee on December 12, 1988, the auditor noted "continuing improvement in the Trust's accounting records and as a result his staff was spending less time in completing their procedure."

Administrative costs in general had decreased. The 1 percent up tick in real estate operating costs over the previous year was negligible, considering inflation and the competitive pressure to please tenants. In this area, HRE welcomed the challenge to excel. "In the near term," declared the Trust in 1989, "our highest priority is to do everything we can to improve our operations: our occupancy, our efficiency, our competitiveness, and the quality of our product and management services."

For HRE to deliver on the promise of a new era it had made to its shareholders, it needed to bargain effectively when negotiating for new properties and write leases that maximized the Trust's advantage, while conceding enough to tenants in a competitive atmosphere to maintain occupancy. In short, among other things, the Trust needed a legal officer. He came aboard in June 1990: Raymond P. Argila. Argila had earned Urstadt's regard while serving as vice president and chief legal officer at Pearce, Urstadt, Mayer & Greer Realty for three years in the mid-1980s, after which he served as senior counsel at the real estate firm of Cushman & Wakefield, Inc., and was also associated with the law firm of Finley, Kumble, Wagner, Heine, Underberg, Manley, Myerson & Casey.

In September 1990, one more member augmented the board of trustees. He was Peter Herrick, vice chairman of the Bank of New York, who among other responsibilities handled the bank's real estate operations.

In 1990, despite HRE's upbeat attitude about the future, the here-and-now snapshot of the present continued to be downbeat, as a serious recession added to the negative factors familiar from the preceding years. The annual report opened with,

> Nineteen Ninety was a year of economic uncertainty, adverse real estate conditions and, unfortunately, substantial reductions in the share prices of most real estate companies. Speculative overbuilding in almost every product type hurt property values everywhere. Demand

was slack because the economy is in recession. The savings and loan disaster caused heavy regulatory pressure on commercial banks, which combined with a weak capital market to nearly stop the flow of new money to real estate.

Lest shareholders mistake this stating of the irreducible facts for a surrender to doom and gloom, the report reminded them that the real estate cycle would inevitably swing upward once again and that HRE, with healthy occupancy rates, and next to no debt, was in a good position to negotiate leases, make acquisitions, and secure bank loans, if necessary, thus suggesting a brighter future.

The battle for control of the REIT, the transition to new management, and a less-than-ideal real estate environment had its effect on HRE's transactions as the 1980s gave way to the 1990s. During the difficult business conditions of the late 1980s and the fight with Kimco, the Trust's buying and selling of properties had slowed. In 1986 it sold its department store in Sterling Heights, Michigan, back to Meijer. "The $7.1 million sale produced a gain of $4.2 million," it reported to shareholders, "which made the sale more attractive than pursuing our development plans."

In 1987, the Trust's strategy was to stand pat. There were no additions to or sales from its portfolio. Its activities included upgrading its office buildings to attract and hold tenants and the minor renovating of its Clearwater, Florida, shopping center. In Manassas, Virginia, its mall-based department store, occupied by Hecht's, a division of May Department Stores, would soon benefit from a major renovation of the mall.

The REIT was also completing a more significant expansion of its Springfield, Massachusetts, shopping center, positioning it to better tap the expanding New England market. Several supermarkets had already shown interest in anchoring the center. That shopping center would also hold pride of place in the Trust's history because in 1990, by dint of an IRS ruling that HRE could directly manage its properties, it became the first retail property that HRE would manage itself.

HRE also made no significant changes to its portfolio in 1988. Fending off Kimco was in the forefront of the REIT's activities. The message to shareholders was that HRE's effective leasing would "position the portfolio for the eventual improvements in markets." Leases signed in 1988 represented three times the space leased in 1987 and overall occupancy throughout the Trust's portfolio was up to 95 percent.

It was in December1989 that the Trust announced its new business plan and its intention of selling off those parts of the portfolio that no longer figured in it. It had already gotten off to a modest start in this direction in October with the first transaction of its new era, the sale of its 105,000-square-foot San Jose, California, Safeway store for $6 million to Pacific Development Associates, an affiliate of Safeway. HRE explained: "Since the lease in place on the property had limited potential over the next several years, we concluded that it did not fit our new strategy. The sale resulted in a capital gain of $3.6 million, or $.60 a share for the Trust in 1989."

Occupancy in its office properties was off in 1989, dropping to 86 percent. But in its Southfield, Michigan, building, Giffels Associates, HRE's main tenant, signed a new ten-year lease accounting for 105,000 square feet of space.

HRE's distribution and service properties had positive news to report. The Chrysler warehouses in Dallas and St. Louis were operating at maximum capacity and the big automobile company wanted to expand the facilities. HRE added a total of more than a hundred thousand square feet to the warehouses. The renovation brought with it about an additional $1 million in rent and figured to boost the Trust's cash flow by about $400,000 annually. Chrysler, once a major problem tenant for the Trust, was now making a healthy contribution to its bottom line.

HRE's plans to remake itself were reported on page 1 of the *Wall Street Journal* on December 14, 1989. The paper also offered a snapshot of just where the Trust stood after the Safeway deal: "HRE has 24 U.S. properties, of which 44% are offices, 41% are retail outlets and shopping centers, and 15% are industrial." It was a picture that would change substantially over the next decade.

The next properties to be sold off, in 1990, were the Kmart stores in Drayton Plains, Michigan, and Citrus Heights, California. They brought in a total of $4.9 million in cash, and the $1.1 million profit they gained for the Trust translated to $.20 a share. "We are also actively seeking to buy property in the East and have looked at hundreds of proposals in 1990," HRE's CEO told shareholders. "We are well positioned to move when we find appropriate investments."

In the next year's annual report, Urstadt led off his message "To Our Shareholders" with some hard but straight talk. "This has been a frustrating year—as frustrating a year as I can remember in my 40 years in the business," he noted. "Nearly every market in the nation has become difficult for real estate investors, and all property types have been adversely affected."

Through these hard times, HRE had been doing better than most REITs, thanks to the fact that it did not overpay for investments when times seemed flush, had not gotten deeply into debt, and had kept occupancy rates fairly high in four of its six office properties. But "falling rents" in 1991 were as much a problem for HRE as for other real estate firms, and its occupancy rate for office space declined by almost 5 percent.

America was in the grip of a tenacious recession, and one direct consequence for HRE was that the anchor tenant in its Springfield, Massachusetts, shopping center, Channel Home Centers, which had occupied fifty thousand square feet of space, vacated when its parent company went bankrupt.

Nevertheless, cash flow increased at HRE's Clearwater, Florida, shopping center, where leasing was on the upswing; and two new restaurants were among the tenants. Elsewhere, a Sears store and a Red Lobster restaurant had been added to the Newington, New Hampshire, location.

HRE Properties at this time added to its board of trustees Robert R. Douglass. Douglass was vice chairman of the Chase Manhattan Bank, where he oversaw the bank's real estate activities. In addition to a distinguished career in finance and banking, Robert Douglass was also experienced in the public realm, having served as a chief of staff to New York State's governor Nelson A. Rockefeller for several years.

By 1991, HRE's operating costs had been under control for four straight years, remaining essentially flat. An example of the Trust's continuing commitment to keeping this string going may be seen in the minutes of the trustees meeting of March 1, 1991. Urstadt's agenda was cost control. "He noted that the staff has completed a review of the trust's real estate taxes, management and insurance costs and has been successful in containing or lowering these significant cost components." Further efficiencies could be anticipated from the REIT's decision to repurchase "odd lots" of fewer than one hundred shares, the accounts of which were expensive to service.

One number that came up at this meeting was certainly pleasing. It was noted that FFO was up almost 8 percent from the previous year. Another pleasing number in 1991 was the approximately $3 million HRE would get from selling the mortgage it held on the Meijer property in Sterling Heights, Michigan. That sum and the even greater one it would derive from refinancing one of its office properties would enhance its cash position as HRE prepared to begin adding those shopping centers it had promised to acquire for its portfolio.

With the assembling of that cash to support its program of acquisitions, HRE was truly about to embark on the beginning of a new era. It was perhaps symbolic of the break it was making with its past that near the end of 1991, during the trustees meeting on November 12, the trustees authorized their CEO to buy out the employment and consulting contract of the REIT's former president, William F. Murdoch.

The New Era Begins in Earnest

At the end of 1990, the expression "core business" made its first appearance in the minutes of a trustees meeting (on December 8). In the 1991 annual report, in a paragraph that seems in hindsight almost an aside, given its future significance, HRE embodied that expression in a momentous transaction, reporting, "the Trust has contracted to buy an attractive small shopping center in Westchester County, north of New York City, on which we expect to close shortly." The three-year-old shopping center would be the REIT's first acquisition in the plan that Urstadt had laid out in 1989, one that foreshadowed Urstadt Biddle's portfolio and operations today.

The New York Times, on March 5, 1992, carried the story of the closing on the property: "HRE Properties said yesterday that it had acquired Heritage 202 Center, a shopping center in Somers, N.Y., from the Heritage Hills Development Corporation for $3.4 million." The shopping center fitted HRE's guidelines for location and property type, but it also represented two additional characteristics of the REIT's future acquisitions. One was that HRE would be concentrating on buying shopping centers in one of the most affluent areas of the United States: Westchester and Putnam counties, suburbs of New York City, and Fairfield County in Connecticut. When buying retail properties, it certainly couldn't hurt to go where the money was, even if the stores were oriented toward the basics.

The second characteristic, true of some but not all of the properties the REIT would acquire, was not so demographically obvious, but partly followed from the fact of affluence. It could be summed up in one word: NIMBY, "not in my backyard."

Shopping centers represented a fairly large-scale development in any community. Development created jobs, raised the value of real estate, provided new amenities, and was healthy for a community's tax base. However, some people saw development as a two-edged sword. Breadwinners who were already at least several rungs up on the corporate ladder often headed the families that moved to these areas. Many of them lived in ample homes on spacious lots. They were sensitive about too many commercial and industrial incursions into a countryside dotted with hills, woods, and all other manner of nature's bounty. They were likely to be well educated and politically savvy and willing to get involved enough with community affairs to see to it that the communities they lived in remained as close to bucolic as possible. They were, after all, putting up with a daily commute to the city so they could return in the evening and for weekends to something that was just the opposite from urban hustle and bustle.

In other words, there was always going to be a pretty strict limit to how much development would be permitted in many of the suburbs of New York City, except for urban areas in those suburbs, such as White Plains, New Rochelle, Yonkers, and Stamford. And if you limit development, putting a cap on how many retail properties can be added, you limit competition. HRE would thus sometimes be buying into areas where the REIT would not have to worry too much about rival shopping centers appearing just down the road in a year or two.

In Somers, the site of HRE's new acquisition, there would never be more than three modest shopping centers in the entire area; and ultimately, HRE would own all of them. This pleasant town of sixty thousand was forced to confront the NIMBY issue beginning in the early 1980s.

First came Pepsico, in 1982, with its plans for offices on Route 100, where between one and two thousand employees would work. IBM followed the next year, with plans for a headquarters two miles down the same road from Pepsico that would ultimately be a workplace for upward of five thousand. By mid-decade, as one person put it in a *New York Times* interview on March 30, 1986, people were beginning to feel as if they were living "under siege."

Then, in the spring of 1986, that part of Somers that did not have the convenient nearby shopping that many people wanted moved to remedy that situation. There already was a smaller Somers Shopping Center in another part of the town, and many people in the area wanted to hold it to just that one.

In 1973, the Heritage Hills Development Corporation, from which HRE would buy their shopping center, had begun a thousand-acre adults-only condominium development in Somers, featuring white single-story units built into a hillside with steep-graded roads. Heritage Hills had 1,300 units in 1986, with space for another 3,100. It was time for a shopping center. Among its tenants would be a medical center, badly needed by Heritage Hills' aging population. As it now stood, the development's residents often had to travel to White Plains or Mt. Kisco for their shopping needs. They were "well off, educated, knowledgeable and want quality services," the developer maintained.

Nearby, Route 100 was already going to house Pepsico and IBM, opponents of additional development countered. Roads would need widening, and nearby historic Colonial and Victorian houses would be overwhelmed. One resident feared that teenagers would hang out at the center. Between the center and the new office structures, too many people might be "wandering around the community," a member of the town board speculated.

The Heritage 202 Center, at the entrance to the Heritage Hills Development, was built with compromises to meet objections. The important point, though, was that future development would be carefully scrutinized. HRE would thus be adding to its portfolio a property where historic forces militated against much more development. It was a retail environment unlike the West and Southwest, where the Trust had previously concentrated its holdings, where restrictive commercial zoning was sometimes akin to a dirty word.

HRE's 1992 annual report celebrated the benefits of shopping center ownership, citing that this type of property benefited "from direct management of tenant mix, promotions and physical appearance." On March 3, 1993, in an act both symbolic and celebratory, HRE's board of trustees would hold its quarterly meeting at a restaurant in the Heritage Hills Shopping Center. At that meeting, Chairman Urstadt, whose business sense has never precluded the timely display of a sense of humor, advised the board that he had glanced into his crystal ball and saw some bad news in the offing, including "bankruptcies and foreclosures." After pausing a beat, he added: "The good news is you'll get used to it."

At the end of 1992, the REIT augmented its roster of Northeastern shopping centers with a new one in Wayne, New Jersey, in an acquisition negotiated by acquisitions director John Kent. HRE bought the Valley Ridge Shopping Center in November from Phillips International, Inc., for $12.3 million, part of which was from a nonrecourse first mortgage of $9.1 million. The ninety-eight-thousand-square-foot complex of retail and office space covered nine acres and had been expanded only two years previously. It was the Trust's first foray into the northern New Jersey market. Anchored by an A&P supermarket and including a branch of the Midlantic Bank and a US post office, the center was already 95 percent leased up.

Acquisitions, by their nature, very often make the biggest impression on shareholders because they are dramatic and new. But leasing is as much an integral part of a REIT's activity; and in 1992, one lease in particular—in its Newington, New Hampshire, mixed-use facility—highlighted HRE's progress.

The Newington property itself was a work in progress, still on its way via renovation and retenanting over a span of several years, from an industrial facility to a mixed office-and-retail development. But now the lease rather than bricks, mortar, and wallboard held the spotlight as HRE announced that Fabri-Centers of America, Inc., was taking 22,500 square feet at Newington. Altogether the lease would be worth about $2.4 million to the Trust, or $0.04 per share annually. Bryant Young, who was promoted that year to senior vice president for Asset Management, negotiated it.

Fabri-Centers had more than six hundred fabric stores in locations throughout the United States, accounting for about $400 million in sales annually. Many of them were named Jo-Ann Fabrics, including the store destined for Newington. The stores carried craft supplies as well as fabrics, and by their nature—as part of the do-it-yourself approach to clothing—were likely to continue to do well even in hard times.

Fabri-Centers, like HRE, was going through some basic changes. The industry of which it was a part was experiencing an extended period of consolidation. Fabri-Centers' Jo-Ann Fabrics stores had been evolving from small stores in enclosed malls to larger outlets in strip malls. One financial analyst, looking at the company in 1992, commented on the appeal of the Jo-Ann stores: "As the world becomes increasingly mechanized and sophisticated, there is a bigger place for the simpler joys like sewing, cooking and fixing up the house." Overall, Fabri-Centers and HRE were a good match.

In fact, Jo-Ann Fabrics was the centerpiece of a veritable blossoming of leases at Newington in 1992. The year began with only 38 percent of the facility's space tenanted; but by 1993, 80 percent, or forty-two thousand square feet, would be leased up.

Financially the Trust was mostly on solid ground in 1992, except in its office properties, where occupancy was down to 81 percent, 8 percent below the previous year. As previously noted, as a matter of company policy, the HRE dividend had been reduced to a more realistic level, amounting to $1.16 per share in 1992, compared to the previous year's $1.40. Net income was down, but 1991's figure had been inflated by the sale of property. In 1992, FFO was a healthy $7,862,000, up slightly from 1991, bolstered by $960,000 from the sale of HRE's Los Angeles shopping center. (While the Trust may have been on solid ground, one could not say the same for that Los Angeles property. Within days of the sale, the shopping center sustained minor damage in an earthquake!) Also this year, the Urstadt family increased its HRE holdings to 19 percent of shares outstanding with the purchase of 125,000 more shares.

In addition to Bryant Young's promotion, John Kent was promoted to vice president for Acquisitions of HRE Properties, and Joyce Mawhinney became the first woman to hold the title of vice president at the Trust. Stephen C. Hagen, a holdover from the Hubbard days, resigned. And George Conklin, the last of the original trustees of Hubbard Real Estate Investments, chose not to stand for reelection. With his departure went the last tie to the Trust's beginning.

By 1993, HRE felt it had made enough of a start toward implementing its business plan to display pie charts in its annual report depicting an evolving REIT. There had now been five major acquisitions since 1989 and eight dispositions. The geographical balance could clearly be seen to be swinging northeastward and toward the ownership of shopping centers.

The text in the annual report spelled out the change: "In 1989, more than half the net book value of our assets was located in the Midwest or West. As of this writing, 66% of this value is concentrated in the East. In 1989, retail property represented only 38% of our net book value. Today, this portion of the portfolio represents almost 65%."

Also dramatic was a bar chart showing the annual increase in gross leasable area under HRE's direct management. There had been small gradual increases from 1989 through 1992, when the figure hit just over five hundred thousand square feet. But in 1993, the number virtually doubled, with just under a million square feet directly under HRE control.

New additions to the Trust's portfolio were shopping centers in Meriden, Connecticut, and Farmingdale (Long Island), New York, bought near the end of the year. The REIT also acquired a ten-thousand-square-foot small office building in Greenwich, Connecticut, just over the border from New York, about a forty-five-minute ride from New York City by train. These acquisitions represented some very careful "shopping" by HRE, since in 1993 other REITs were augmenting their cash positions through public offerings, priming themselves for expansion and thereby making for a hot acquisitions market.

The Townline Square Shopping Center in Meriden, Connecticut, in New Haven County—just north of the Merritt Parkway and about midway between

Hartford and New Haven, which the Trust purchased on December 22, 1993, from Aetna Life Insurance—was especially significant. First, it cost $25 million, "the largest single purchase in the Trust's history," HRE announced. Of that amount, $10 million came from cash ($5 million of that from a line of credit), and the remaining $15 million from first mortgage financing at 7.5 percent from Aetna. It was also HRE's largest property of its type, adding 290,000 square feet of leasable space on almost thirty acres to the REIT's retail holdings. Featuring a forty-five-thousand-square-foot ShopRite supermarket, the Meriden Center brought with it several major retailers among its twenty tenants, including Marshall's, Bradlees (the largest tenant, with 85,900 square feet), and a fifty-thousand-square-foot Wiz consumer electronics store. (In 1998, following the Wiz's bankruptcy, the space it occupied would be taken by Old Navy and Linens 'n Things.) The shopping center was 95 percent leased up when HRE acquired it.

Located on Route 5, not far from Interstate Highways 91 and 691 in a densely populated area, Townline would tap a local market of about one hundred thousand in this white-collar bedroom community. There were two other shopping centers within two miles of Townline Square, and a total of eight within three miles.

In its first acquisition on Long Island, HRE acquired the Bi-County Shopping Center in Farmingdale on Route 109. For $5.4 million, the Trust added seventy thousand square feet of leasable retail space. Farmingdale, near the border between Nassau and Suffolk counties, is 30 miles east of New York City. A King Kullen Supermarket, a dominant Long Island regional chain started by Michael Cullen in 1930, anchored the shopping center, which opened in 1982. Within six years after he had started the chain, Cullen opened seventeen stores in Queens and on Long Island and the chain flourished after World War II with the movement of population to the suburbs.

HRE was also adding by subtracting, trimming properties from the portfolio that were a drag on the bottom line and no longer squared with its business plan. Office buildings in Portland, Oregon; Charlotte, North Carolina; and Santa Ana, California, that seemed so promising in the early to mid-1980s had gradually come to resemble 525,000 square feet of white elephant. It had become an expensive struggle for HRE to maintain viable occupancy rates. Early in 1993 the occupancy rate in the Portland building was down to 68 percent and cash flow from the property just covered the debt service. Also they were scattered geographically, precluding direct management by the REIT and now that the market for such properties had improved sufficiently, they were sold.

As the Trust explained: "These properties had become drains on our cash flow with little probability of near-term improvement. All of them were subject to nonrecourse mortgages with high debt service charges, and there were the additional costs of tenant improvements, commissions and other expenses related to leasing office space. By disposing of these properties—and taking a one-time noncash charge against earnings—we have been able to eliminate this continuing drain."

The office buildings that HRE retained—in Southfield, Michigan; Houston; and Denver—were debt free. The Denver property, in a real estate environment where Urstadt had spotted the overbuilding early on, was still a problem, with half its space unoccupied. This situation was aggravated in 1993 when thirty-four thousand square feet became vacant when a tenant did not renew its lease. But there were "prospective" tenants in the offing, and the future looked brighter there.

The 1993 net loss of almost $5 million can be attributed to the Trust's sale of the office buildings in Portland, Charlotte, and Santa Ana, which resulted in noncash charges of over $8 million. The joint venture in the buildings in Portland and Charlotte was in default of mortgage loans, and HRE had written down the carrying value of its net investment in them to zero. The partnership with Santa Anita Realty—it was called Hubanita—no longer made sense for HRE. The office market in Southern California had weakened. To improve leasing would have required an influx of cash that the Trust could better employ elsewhere. So HRE sold its interest in the venture to its partner.

But that was only a part of the story for 1993. The more telling funds from operations rose $0.03 per share compared to the previous year—the mark of a good, not troubling, fiscal year.

Joining HRE Proprieties in 1993 as a vice president in the Asset Management Group was Willing "Wing" Biddle. Before he came to HRE, the thirty-three-year-old Biddle, Charles J. Urstadt's son-in-law, served as a second vice president at Chase Manhattan Bank in the real estate division and also completed a four-year period as a vice president at Levites Realty Management Corp., a New York City developer. Also joining the Trust during this period was Thomas D. Myers. He became associate counsel in 1995 and remains with the company to this day.

In 1994, the Trust's silver anniversary, HRE Properties had virtually nothing but good news to report. In place of the cautious projection of modest progress, at best, for itself amidst a minefield of overbuilding, recession, and uncooperative interest rates that had characterized the note "To Our Shareholders" in the past five annual reports, the 1994 report heralded a "resounding recovery." The Trust now boldly characterized itself as a "retail REIT." Its dividend was up $0.04 a share, FFO rose again, the REIT's asset base had grown, new properties boosted revenues, and all of this had happened while costs remained stable. Twenty-five years after two mortgage bankers, John and Morry Hubbard, founded Hubbard Real Estate Investments for Merrill Lynch, their REIT went by a different name and was "a different and stronger company," stated HRE. But one thing hadn't changed since the first few months of the Trust's existence: it still had not missed a single quarterly dividend.

While the 1994 annual report briefly gazed back at HRE Properties' past, the bulk of what it had to say spoke very much to the future; and looking forward, the theme continued to be shopping centers. As in 1993, the most significant addition to the Trust's portfolio was a property in Connecticut. HRE bought the Danbury Square Shopping Center in Danbury for $20 million from Aetna Life Insurance Company—$8 million in cash and the rest in a first mortgage from Aetna at 9.5 percent—closing on it on January 6, 1995. The location of this 193,000-square-foot "power center" on twenty acres next to the Danbury Fair Mall, with which it shared a ring road for access, gave it significant potential for rewarding a company that could keep it leased up with the right mix of tenants. HRE anticipated spending about $700,000 on improvements to Danbury Square in the coming year. With only a 5 percent vacancy rate, the center boasted such familiar stores as Barnes & Noble, Toys"R"Us (65,000 square feet), and Bed Bath & Beyond among its twenty-three tenants, 80 percent of whom were national retailers with solid credit ratings. It also had a Loehmann's, a widely popular off-price women's clothing store. In 1996, Mikasa, a major player in the tabletop wares industry, would take 20,000 square feet.

The local customer base seemed just right: Danbury in 1994 was a white-collar, bedroom community with a population of sixty-five thousand and median household income of $71,866. HRE's Danbury Square Shopping Center, which opened in 1989, was also near Interstate Route 84, providing easy access to shoppers from nearby New York State. In addition to the 1.2-million-square-foot Danbury Fair Mall, Connecticut's largest mall, another nearby draw for shoppers was a Stew Leonard's gourmet food emporium.

At its shopping center in Springfield, Massachusetts, as at its Newington mixed-use facility in New Hampshire, HRE had closed its on-site property management offices and was now managing both directly from its New York headquarters. This move reduced costs and helped to build up the in-house expertise the REIT would need to maximize profits from acquisitions to come. By the end of the year, the Trust would be directly managing over a million square feet in nine properties.

HRE also acquired in 1994 another small office building in Greenwich, Connecticut, near the one it had bought the previous year. The buildings were not far from the Metro-North train station, and Greenwich itself was just off Interstate 95.

Although it had not yet closed on the deal, HRE had contracted to sell its Chrysler warehouses at the end of 1994. Comparing a list of their locations with the locations in which the Trust was buying shopping centers gives a good sense of how rapidly HRE was now moving from a REIT with a mix of industrial, office, and retail properties scattered across America to one that could be accurately described as a shopping center REIT focused on the Northeast. Those Chrysler warehouses were scattered in Denver, Memphis, Orlando, and Portland, Oregon; and when HRE closed on them, it would be a REIT with 71 percent of its value in retail properties.

In discussing in its annual report the significance of the transactions it had made in 1994, HRE gave its most detailed description yet of the rationale behind its business strategy:

> First, geographic concentration enhances management's knowledge of markets and individual properties from the vantage of both acquisitions and operations. It enlarges the Trust's presence within its markets, which helps to lease space, retain tenants, lower costs and identify new opportunities for investment. It makes better use of management resources and increases management's overall responsiveness, efficiency and control. The economic region within a 75-mile radius of New York City, where all the recent Trust acquisitions have occurred, is the country's largest established market with 7.7 million households and one of the nation's highest median household incomes.
>
> Second, concentration on shopping centers sharpens management's proficiency in investing in and operating this property type. Over time, the community shopping center has proven to be a rewarding and exceptionally resilient investment which, when skillfully and aggressively managed, will gradually increase in value. Shopping centers in which the Trust invests offer convenience and basic goods and services, attributes that make them less vulnerable to economic cycles and the vagaries of retailing. The Trust's centers are usually supermarket-anchored, well-positioned competitively within their markets and supported by strong suburban demographics.
>
> There are additional advantages to owning shopping centers. Operating expenses are almost wholly rechargeable to the tenants which enables substantial recovery of costs and offers protection against inflation. Percentage rent provisions allow participation in tenant's sales above a certain level; this income can be substantial as sales grow over time, whether driven by real growth, inflation or both. As with all operating properties, the turnover of leases enables rental income generally to keep current with the market.

HRE acknowledged also the possible downside of the turn it had taken. The regional economy could dip, whereas geographical diversity spreads that risk. But all things considered, the direction it had decided to go seemed sensible; and in the few years since the Trust had begun to transform itself, the results had confirmed that conclusion. The next decade would underline the wisdom of this course of action.

Meanwhile, although earmarked for eventual disposition, HRE's office properties in Denver; Southfield, Michigan; and Houston were still in the portfolio. And the Trust was exerting its maximum effort to see to it that they contributed to the company's cash flow until the time was right to sell them. The Denver building, in particular, was a cause for satisfaction because the building's previous year's 50 percent occupancy rate had now been drastically improved with only a 5 percent vacancy rate. One new tenant, Multifoods, had accounted for thirty thousand square feet of the sixty-two thousand that was filled during the year. The Houston and Southfield properties were performing satisfactorily as well.

What did all this activity add up to? Some very nice numbers, including an FFO that in 1994 rose 13 percent over the previous year's, enabling the dividend to increase by $0.02 a share to $1.10. When the quarterly dividend was bumped up to $0.28 a share in June, it was the first such upward move since 1986.

By any measure, HRE in the mid-1990s was a REIT on the move. In 1995, it even made a literal move. Cutting loose from Merrill Lynch and the Hubbard Advisory Corporation had left HRE's headquarters still in Manhattan, on fashionable and expensive Fifth Avenue, where the REIT was paying $63 per square foot for its space. With the Trust's emphasis on building a portfolio of properties located in New York City's northern and northeastern suburbs, it made less and less sense every year for HRE to maintain its headquarters in the heart of Gotham. Its recent purchase of office space in Greenwich, Connecticut, presented the inviting possibility of relocating to a place that was even closer to its core properties while offering savings on its office rent in the bargain. Consequently, HRE in 1995 moved its corporate headquarters to its two-story office building with basement level parking at 321 Railroad Avenue in Greenwich, Connecticut, for which it paid $75 per square foot, where it occupied the top floor and leased the ground floor to a tenant. HRE's board of trustees held their first meeting there on June 7, 1995.

At the end of 1994, HRE had hired Leslie Larsen as director of Property Sales to market its noncore assets. Now, from its new headquarters, HRE made a formal announcement that reinforced its stated intention five years previously to make a major disposition of its noncore properties. The difference was that this time, over the course of several years, the Trust hoped to clean the slate of all holdover properties from the Hubbard era, using the proceeds to reinvest in its core properties. The *Wall Street Journal* carried the story on September 15, 1995, reporting that a revaluation of the properties that HRE had announced its intention to sell would result in a nonrecurring, noncash charge of $7 million for the Trust in its third quarter.

HRE spelled out its intentions in its 1995 annual report, stating its belief "that economic conditions in the real estate markets where the Trust's non-core properties are located have improved and that opportunities to sell those properties over the next several years have also improved. At October 31, 1995, the non-core properties total eleven properties, having an aggregate net book value of $6,212,000 and comprise all of the Trust's office (with the exception of the Trust's headquarters), distribution and service facilities, and certain retail properties located outside the Northeastern region of the United States."

At the end of the previous year, HRE had sold four of its Chrysler warehouses. The capital gains on this sale amounted to about $7.5 million and added $13 million in cash that the Trust could apply to the purchase of new core properties. Another infusion of cash came from the disposition of the Hecht's department store in Manassas, Virginia, which would produce at the sale's close on January 4, 1996, capital gains of over $6 million. Negotiations already were underway as 1995 ended for the sale of HRE's Houston office building.

The next significant use of its trove of cash was HRE's purchase in 1995 of the ShopRite Plaza in Carmel, New York. In suburban Putnam County, not far from HRE's new headquarters in Greenwich, Carmel had a local population of about thirty thousand. The 126,000-square-foot, nineteen-acre shopping center, built in 1983, came with twelve tenants—and only 4 percent of its space vacant—and was anchored by a ShopRite supermarket and Fay's Drug Store.

The ShopRite supermarket chain was started in New Jersey in 1946 as a cooperative formed by seven independent grocers who were having trouble competing with the major supermarket chains. They adopted the name ShopRite in 1951; by then there were fifty member stores. In the 1960s, one group of stores split off to form the Pathmark chain. The ShopRite chain continued to grow, and today it is the largest retailer-owned cooperative in America. It operates in five states in the Northeast and employ upward of fifty thousand.

With the acquisition of the ShopRite Plaza in Carmel, the retail sector of HRE's assets now represented 77 percent of its holdings, up from 38 percent in 1989. HRE now had just under two hundred tenants in all of its properties. A good deal of time and energy at the REIT was going into analyzing properties in its core market for possible acquisition. Leasing and, increasingly, managing its properties was time-consuming. It was a process that required rationalization and control; and toward that end, in March 1994, Willing Biddle reported to the board of trustees that he was putting together a *Property Management Manual* "which would establish uniform policies and procedures relating to the operation of Trust properties."

Newly appointed Chief Executive Officer Charles J. Urstadt gets down to work.

The Jo-Ann Fabrics store at the Trust's Newington, New Hampshire location, where renovation and re-tenanting over a span of several years turned an industrial facility into a mixed office and retail development.

HRE acquired the Townline Square Shopping Center in Meriden, Connecticut in 1993.

The Christmas Tree Shops at Danbury Square. HRE bought the shopping center in Danbury, Connecticut for $20 million from Aetna Life Insurance Company in 1994.

The ShopRite Plaza in Carmel, New York. Typical of the Company's shopping centers, it's anchored by a supermarket.

The building in Greenwich, Connecticut, purchased in 1994, that became the Company's headquarters the following year.

The Eastchester Mall in White Plains, New York, was a "DownREIT" acquisition, in which the seller gained the advantage of tax deferment.

Amazingly, the company was carrying out its operations with a total only of sixteen employees! There's one clue to HRE's ability to keep its operating and managerial costs level from year to year. The new property and management information system that it set up in 1995 and brought online the following year was another contributing factor.

As of December 31, 1995, there were 2,819 shareholders of record of the Trust's common shares, which traded in the $13-$15 range. The shareholders received a dividend of $1.14 per share for 1995, up from the previous year in spite of the toll on some of HRE's tenants that the unfavorable retail environment had taken during the year. Caldor—a major tenant in the Trust's Springfield, Massachusetts, shopping center—was in bankruptcy, but still operating. Bradlees and Jamesway, significant tenants in other of the Trust's properties, were also in bankruptcy; but one of the bankruptcies had long been anticipated and a third party had guaranteed the other company's credit. On the whole, the financial picture was favorable, with funds from operations up a healthy 13 percent.

One footnote to HRE's history is worth noting here. Operating and growing a REIT, as with any business, is far from a magical practice; and sometimes a company makes a move that just doesn't quite work out. For some time at trustee meetings, there had been discussion about the possibility of opening a subsidiary operation in which the Trust would use its developing management expertise to manage properties for other firms. In 1995, HRE undertook to manage a four-hundred-thousand-square-foot shopping center in Syracuse for a major financial institution. The 1995 annual report said the Trust "will seek additional property management and leasing business as a means to increase income, create acquisition opportunities and spread overhead costs over an even greater asset base." While the Trust made money managing the property, the experience showed it was wiser to only manage properties within the Trust's target acquisition market.

The year 1996 saw HRE reduce its debt by $19 million while raising its dividend for the third straight year. Another positive was that A&P opened a new sixty-four-thousand-square-foot Super Foodmart at HRE's Five Town Plaza center in Springfield, Massachusetts. In addition, the space occupied by Jamesway, which had filed for bankruptcy at the Trust's Carmel, New York Center, was re-leased to a movie theater, health club, and other small tenants.

By 1996, the Trust and its strategic plan were doing so well that management was more than willing to be compared head to head with "the big boys." On page 3 of its 1996 annual report, HRE presented a bar chart that compared its total average annual return (dividends plus change in stock price) with that of the five largest shopping center REITs. Of the five—New Plan, Vornado, Kimco, Weingarten, and Federal—only Vornado, with a capitalization approximately fourteen times that of HRE, held its own with HRE. Big may have been beautiful, said the Trust, but "little is lovely." Or to put it more bluntly, HRE declared, "Size is Vanity—Profits Are Sanity."

This comparison notwithstanding, the Trust's share price was not yet truly reflecting its performance. It was a source of persistent irritation that for some time the "analysts" seemed to have consistently underrated and overlooked, if not totally misrepresented, HRE's operation and prospects. In 1992, for example, the board of trustees had examined the draft of a research report on the Trust prepared by Green Street Advisors and, according to the minutes of the board's meeting on September 16, concluded "that the draft report was biased, filled with innuendo and contained factual inaccuracies." Nevertheless, Green Street published its report substantially as it appeared in the draft. More typically, driven mostly by the concerns of institutional investors, whose criterion of big numbers at this time precluded more than a second glance at a strong small cap performer, the "analysts" paid little or no heed to HRE.

One analyst thought HRE was so lacking in pizzazz and so far behind the times that he labeled it a "dinosaur." The next day, HRE's staff came into the office to find toy dinosaurs planted throughout the premises, Charles Urstadt's way of commenting on the commentator. (While HRE would continue to evolve, that analyst has not been heard from for some time and may now be extinct.)

Despite the nay-sayers, "the little engine that could" kept picking up steam. For the fourth straight year, the REIT's funds from operations were up in 1996, by a healthy 12 percent, to $1.78 per share. In fact, the annual rate of FFO growth was above 10 percent over that four-year span. The annual dividend per share increased $0.08 from the previous year to $1.24. The year 1996 also marked a new high in total revenues at $24.4 million.

And in 1996, seeking to make the most of its undervalued share price, the board approved a plan to repurchase a million of its shares. As the minutes of the May 2 meeting recorded: "Mr. Urstadt noted that the Trust's share price has traded in a narrow range for several years, is undervalued in the market and at current prices represents a good investment of Trust funds."

Several of the HRE transactions in 1996 demonstrate that management was seeking profitable ventures in any form they might present themselves, even if they didn't go completely according to plan. At the end of the year, a bit into fiscal 1997, the Trust even made a deal with its erstwhile aggressive suitor, the Kimco Realty Corporation. HRE still owned a large noncore property shopping center in Clearwater, Florida, which, the board of trustees noted, had been under performing, with "chronic tenant vacancies and a weak leasing market." Kimco still owned approximately six hundred thousand shares of HRE it had acquired in its earlier unsuccessful attempt to absorb the Trust. These were the basic elements of a deal. Kimco agreed to contribute its HRE shares to a partnership with HRE, which maintained control as the general partner, in the Clearwater property, with Kimco taking over its management, allowing HRE to concentrate on managing its core properties in the Northeast. Kimco not only had great expertise in managing shopping centers by dint of its vast holdings but had also made Florida its core area for acquisitions, thus sharpening its leasing experience in the Sunshine State. As HRE's CEO Urstadt remarked of the venture, "While this transaction will not have a significant impact on HRE's funds from operations or its financial condition, we expect the cash flow and value of this property to improve the joint ownership and management of the shopping center." It was a classical win-win situation for the former adversaries, the chairmen of which, Charles Urstadt and Milton Cooper, had since become friends.

Also in the spirit of flexibility, HRE departed slightly from its strategic plan in 1996, acquiring for $880,000 a 30,700-foot shopping center, Southern Plaza, next to its Tempe, Arizona, shopping center, which was still anchored by a Mervyns department store. The reasons for this move were simple: the price was right and the added value would make for an even better outcome when HRE eventually disposed of the now-enhanced property. The acquisition was proved right in 2007 when the REIT sold the property for an $11 million profit.

Despite some activity that fell outside the Trust's basic business plan, HRE continued in 1996 to move in the direction in which it had been set under Urstadt's guidance. Nothing epitomized that more than the REIT's sale of its office buildings in Houston, where negotiations for its disposition had gotten underway in the previous year, and in Denver. The average yield of 7.5 percent from these dispositions enabled HRE to lower its mortgage debt, which was running 9.5 percent. It also gave the REIT more cash to spend on new core properties. The Denver sale, where overbuilding in the area had created difficult conditions for many years, was especially satisfying. John C. Merritt of HRE's acquisitions department commented: "The submarket for office buildings such as One Denver Highlands has improved dramatically in the last several years. As a result, we were able to sell our property for the highest sale price per square foot reported in over a decade."

Those transactions left the Trust with only one major office property. In that holding—the Giffels Building in Southfield, Michigan—one tenant, Peregrine, Inc., had just taken seventy thousand square feet of space on a five-year lease, bringing occupancy to a full 100 percent. "Peregrine will take occupancy as the space becomes available," announced Willing Biddle. "This immediate occupancy coupled with favorable lease terms will have a positive impact on HRE's funds from operations." Altogether, HRE was now down to only eight noncore properties with a net book value of $32,986,000.

Geographical consolidation had given the Trust an entirely new look. At one time, a tour of Trust properties would have necessitated use of a corporate jet. But on June 11, 1997, CEO Charles Urstadt would conduct such a tour for his board on a three-hour bus trip, showing them the Heritage 202 Center, the Danbury Square Shopping Center, the Carmel ShopRite Center, and a proposed acquisition in Ridgefield, Connecticut.

The growth and transformation of the Trust had begun when office copiers were just becoming standard equipment and fax machines were still in the future. Serious data processing involved the use of IBM cards on large computers on which smaller companies could only afford to rent time. By 1997, nobody at HRE thought twice about having a personal computer on their desk; and in December of that year, the company was busy having itself checked out for any potential Y2K problems (there were none).

Even a few tenant reversals in the tough retail competitive atmosphere in the Northeast failed to make a significant dent in HRE's ongoing success story. Caldor was still in bankruptcy, but still operating. Herman's—a sporting goods chain, with a store in the Danbury Square Shopping Center—went under; but Sneaker Stadium stepped in to pick up the lease. And the Wiz left at the Townline property in Meriden, Connecticut; and Bradlees filed for bankruptcy, closing its store at that shopping center; but fortunately, the lease was guaranteed by the Stop & Shop Supermarket company, which continued to pay the rent.

The HRE transition from the multiuse HREI to a more specialized retail REIT was now virtually complete. Having positioned the Trust on a solid foundation with a business plan that was moving forward just as it was supposed to, and with the likelihood that it would continue to do so, CEO Urstadt recognized it was time for another change. However this change would not involve the direction of the company, but rather would ensure that the direction would remain largely unchanged, with only the appropriate fine-tuning that any business needs to respond to its competitive environment.

Chapter Five

URSTADT BIDDLE PROPERTIES

Keeping the company on its steady, increasingly prosperous course was the prime task of HRE'S management in the mid-1990s. To this end, continuing the measures it took in the late 1980s to prevent a hostile takeover, HRE made its board of trustees more impregnable to outside interference. In 1993, the board created three classes of trustees with three-year terms of office expiring on a staggered basis. According to HRE, this would "help to insure continuity and stability of the Trust's management." At the beginning of 1995, in another step to prevent a hostile takeover, HRE increased the vote required to remove a trustee to two-thirds of all common shares.

Even more basic measures "to insure continuity and stability" were in the works. The HRE that emerged in the early 1990s was largely the product of the vision and guidance of Charles J. Urstadt. His commitment to the trust's future had by now become embodied in the Urstadt family's substantial holdings of HRE shares. Very conscious of the need to maintain continuity and put in place "the next generation of the company's leadership," Mr. Urstadt—at a meeting of HRE's Compensation Committee on November 6, 1996—recommended that his son-in-law, Willing Biddle, become president of HRE. Following the approval of the trustees, HRE, on December 19, announced that Biddle, at age thirty-five, had become president as well as chief operating officer of the Trust. Urstadt, who remained chairman and CEO, commented: "Wing Biddle has been an integral part of HRE's recent growth, profitability and successful portfolio restructure. He has demonstrated outstanding leadership." The move, Urstadt said, would provide the REIT with "a highly capable and youthful executive team" and "ensure HRE's continued growth and success for many years to come."

On July 10, 1997, the board was enlarged from seven to nine members. Biddle was one of the new members; the other was Charles D. Urstadt, son of the company's chairman. The younger Urstadt, like his father, had substantial experience in the real estate business. He was an executive vice president at

Brown Harris Stevens and had been the publisher of *New York Construction News*, a weekly newspaper that covered construction and real estate activity in the Tri-State metropolitan New York area.

Continuity, given the changing nature of the industry in which it did business, also involved the appropriate modification of the trust to compete in a new environment. For some time, Chairman Urstadt had raised at board meetings the possibility of reorganizing the Trust as a corporation, a measure that a number of REITs were taking. On December 18, 1996, Urstadt had formally proposed such a move for HRE; and on December 26, the board had given its final approval to create HRE Properties, Inc.

Thus the machinery was set in motion and the transformation was completed, after approval at the annual shareholders meeting, at 4:30 PM on March 12, 1997. With the changeover, the 5,346,081 outstanding beneficial shares in the Trust automatically became common stock in the new corporation, which was organized in Maryland. The Trust, merged into the new corporation, ceased to exist as a separate entity. The board met for the last time as trustees of HRE on March 12 and, upon conclusion of their meeting, resumed meeting as directors of the new company. In its press release describing the change, the company stated that "the purpose of the Merger was to modernize the Trust's governance procedures and to provide the Trust with a greater degree of certainty and flexibility in planning and implementing corporate action by adopting a form of organization used by many established real estate investment trusts."

One more significant change was in the offing. Hubbard Real Estate Investments, as the Trust was originally known, had been so named to associate it with the reputation and real estate experience of the Hubbards. Their imprint had remained in the name, HRE. At a board of directors meeting on December 17, 1997, Urstadt—pointing out that at this point in the company's development the HRE label lacked "identity and has been confused with other similarly named real estate companies"—suggested changing HRE to Urstadt Biddle Properties, Inc. The reason for the new name, he said, was "to identify the Company with its current business activities and its principal stockholders and key management and to provide the Company with a more appropriate name which will generate name recognition and improve investor perception." Urstadt also said "that he and Mr. Biddle would consider the use of their names as an endorsement by them of the financial condition and outlook of the Company." With shareholder approval, the new name became official on March 11, 1998; and thus was born the name—and the stock symbol, UBP—under which the company does business today. The name change was heralded on the inside of the front cover of the company's 1998 annual report, where the text began, "Urstadt Biddle Properties, Inc. (formerly HRE Properties, Inc.)."

Growing Urstadt Biddle Properties

The new Maryland corporation formed in 1997 owned eighteen properties in twelve states with about 2,769,000 square feet of gross leasable space. As a retail REIT, it was operating in a sector of the industry that was being slighted by investors, who still gravitated more toward office and industrial properties. But as *Shopping Center World* had pointed out in its issue of October 1, 1997, "Although somewhat lost in the glare of flashier commercial markets, retail REITS have a growth story to tell investors." Characterizing that story was a key word, "Acquisitions." Whether operating as HRE or the soon-to-be Urstadt Biddle Properties, the still small-cap real estate investment trust on Railroad Avenue in Greenwich, Connecticut, was reflecting a very much upbeat part of that story.

As had been its tradition, HRE would continue to grow, slowly but steadily, mining the profitable possibilities in regional shopping centers—supermarkets and big-box retailers such as Bed Bath & Beyond were now competing for limited available space—while trying its best to sidestep the minefields of bankruptcies such as beset discounters Caldor, Bradlees, and Jamesway, so recently a disturbing part of its business environment. As HRE's CFO, James Moore, told *Shopping Center World* in mid-1996, "In community size shopping centers, you will always have turnover of smaller tenants." But more recently, the restructuring of major discounters had become an issue. "You need to be concerned about the viability of national tenants."

That minefield would continue to pose specific dangers in 1997. The Wiz—a once-familiar, omnipresent consumer electronics discounter in the region—was teetering on the edge of bankruptcy. In fact, in the Trust's Townline Square Center in Meriden, where it had been subleasing from another more credit-worthy tenant, the Wiz did go out.

Moving with care, the REIT made a few carefully chosen purchases, one of which was already familiar to CEO Charles Urstadt. In 1981, the Manhattan-based company he headed—Pearce, Urstadt, Mayer & Greer—had sold the Eastchester Mall in White Plains, New York, to Sutom Corporation for $3.7 million. At the very end of 1996, Urstadt renewed his connection to that mall when HRE became a general partner in the property through a "DownREIT" acquisition, in which the seller gained the advantage of tax deferment. HRE exchanged stock for the property, with the seller becoming a limited partner. Given the avid competition for good properties in the area and their generally low turnover rate, HRE hoped to be able to offer such deals to potential sellers in the future, thus expanding its potential pool of acquisitions.

The sixty-eight-thousand-square-foot, 100 percent-leased Eastchester Mall—located on Route 22 near the thriving communities of Bronxville, Scarsdale, and Tuckahoe in a densely populated, affluent part of New York's Westchester County—became the second smallest in the Trust's portfolio, bigger only than the one in Somers. One of A&P's Food Emporium supermarkets, an upscale store known for its specialty gourmet products, anchored the mall. The chain had begun as part of Shopwell and was acquired by A&P in 1986.

As in previous years, Urstadt Biddle did not hesitate to step outside its business plan when it was advantageous to the Trust. Late in 1997, the REIT added to its portfolio a nine-acre parcel in Jonesboro, Georgia, home to a 117,000-square-foot department store that was net-leased to Value City Department Stores, Inc. The acquisition was anything but routine. Thirteen years prior, in 1974, the Trust had participated in the property's transfer and mortgage financing, providing $143,000 toward the acquisition cost of the Jonesboro property and securing the loan with a mortgage. In connection with the payoff of that mortgage loan in 1996, the REIT's assistant counsel Thomas Myers discovered among the original documentation that the Trust also had acquired, and retained, an option to purchase the property. When the Trust exercised that option, the property owner commenced litigation to challenge the option's enforceability. Within the year, the matter was settled; and the property acquired at a cost of $375,000 over the outstanding mortgage balance, a total investment of $2.27 million. At the time, Willing Biddle reported to the directors that the settlement would yield a "going in return" in excess of 13 percent on an all cash basis on the REIT's investment. His estimate proved conservative. Within five years, the property would be sold for $3.3 million.

Around this time, Biddle's own attention to detail produced a similar gain. While perusing the REIT's noncompete clause with Mervyns, the Arizona department store, he discovered that Mervyns had violated a section that permitted HRE to recover a share of their sales amounting to about $3 million.

Leasing and upgrading also contributed substantially to the company's long-term prosperity in 1996. For example, at the Newington, New Hampshire, mixed-use facility, the expiration of a nonretail lease allowed HRE to bring in a branch of the Big Party! Stores at a higher rent than the 8,500 square feet of space had been delivering. Three years later, the Big Party! chain of stores would go bankrupt, but their leases and businesses would pass into the hands of the iParty Corporation, with no negative impact on the REIT.

Renovation and upgrading, in which the company added value to acquisitions through better management and maintenance of property, were reinforced in 1998 with the addition of Wayne Wirth as vice president for Management and Construction. He arrived just in time. During the year, UBP renovated three of its shopping centers: the Carmel ShopRite Center, Five Town Plaza, and the Ridgefield Center. With his twenty-five years of experience in the field, Wirth's presence enlarged the potential pool of acquisitions to include centers that might need substantial work to make them productive properties.

Wirth had demonstrated his knack for taking the initiative in everything he did. When his young daughter took an interest in beekeeping at their new home in Wappingers Falls, New York, he set about making himself an expert on the subject. His ad in a local paper—"New beekeeper in town needs advice and tools"—quickly brought assistance, and he and his daughter were on their way with a new hobby.

In 1998, the theme of continuity prevailed in the company's financial figures as well as its management and mission. It was a bad period for REIT stock prices—NAREIT's All REIT index lost 18.8 percent—but UBP held the decrease on its total return to stockholders to just 6.7 percent and continued to increase FFO by about 10 percent per year. The UBP portfolio as a whole was 96 percent leased, and acquisitions continued apace in the company's target area. As the company's 1998 annual report to stockholders, reflecting its chairman's nautical background, colorfully put it, "Although the tide went out on REITs your 'ship' still has plenty of water under its keel." In fact, all told that report characterized 1998 as a "banner year."

Growing the company required more capital. With the conclusion of its $35 million privately placed preferred stock sale on January 9, 1998, UBP garnered its first major corporate credit rating (BB-), an achievement still unusual for a REIT, especially a relatively small one. The issue was priced at 8.99 percent and was noncallable by the issuer for ten years. "We believe this preferred stock issue represents the first privately placed perpetual preferred stock offering made by a real estate investment trust and marks HRE's re-entrance into the capital markets," remarked CEO Urstadt. "The additional source of capital will increase the company's equity base by nearly a third and reduce our already low debt to total capitalization ratio to about 15%. We are actively seeking new acquisitions in our Northeast target area and we plan to utilize these funds in the near term at spreads positive to the cost of capital."

UBP also declared a one-for-one stock dividend in June through the issuance of a new class of common stock; and on December 11, the REIT sold 162,500 shares of the new shares of this Class A common stock in a private placement for $1.3 million. According to Urstadt, "the new class of common stock is intended to, among other things, provide flexibility to the Company to raise additional equity, finance the future growth of the Company and provide increased liquidity for our capital stock. Also, we can utilize the new Class A common stock as consideration for property acquisitions without diluting the ownership interests of our existing stockholders." Taking into account the stock dividend, the year produced a gain of 12.5 percent in the dividend rate to $1.28 per common share, a rate that was still under 70 percent of annual FFO.

The company was, indeed, "actively seeking new acquisitions" that year—seeking and finding them. During this period, UBP would spend about $40 million, adding three hundred thousand square feet of leasable space to its portfolio. The stock sale helped to finance the purchase of yet another shopping center in UBP's target area, this time on Route 9 in Westchester County's Briarcliff Manor-Ossining area. Nearby communities include North Tarrytown, Pleasantville, and Scarborough. Again using a DownREIT partnership that put UBP in control, the company added the Arcadian Shopping Center for $11.5 million. The seller contributed the property to the partnership, subject to a $6.3 million mortgage. A few months later, in February 1999, UBP augmented this acquisition with the cash purchase of a twenty-eight-thousand-square-foot retail property including four acres of land adjacent to the center for $1.9 million.

UBP president Willing Biddle remarked of the DownREIT transaction: "This is of great benefit to owners who are reluctant to sell because of the federal and state taxes associated with capital gains due upon the sale of their property. It also represents an advantage to UBP because we can offer an economically attractive solution to an owner's potential tax problem."

Anchoring the 145,000-square-foot, 98 percent-leased Arcadian Shopping Center, which had been built in the 1970s on a twelve-acre property, was a sixty-five-thousand-square-foot Stop & Shop Supermarket. Among other tenants were CVS Drugs, an M&T Bank, McDonald's, and Toy Works.

In this period, UBP aggressively zeroed in on affluent, densely populated Fairfield County, Connecticut, and Westchester County, New York—all a short drive from the company's Greenwich headquarters. As Charles Urstadt was to put it in an article he wrote for *Real Estate Weekly* in 2001: "If you wanted to locate the concept of affluence on a map of the United States, sticking pins in Westchester and Fairfield Counties would be a good start. But there's more than wealth here in the heartland of suburbia—there's a huge market noted for its stability in population and spending."

One of UBP's acquisitions in this area involved downtown retail properties rather than a full shopping center. The company purchased a block of stores, offices, and a few apartments in the heart of charming downtown Ridgefield, Connecticut, voted the state's number 1 town, and almost immediately raised occupancy in them by renovating the properties and upgrading the tenant roster. The investment was prudent because the town, the site of an important battle in the American Revolution, had seen significant growth and building over the past three decades.

Also in Connecticut in 1998, on September 9, UBP closed on the acquisition of the Goodwives Shopping Plaza, which company Director of Acquisitions John Merrit characterized as "the pre-eminent shopping center in the affluent community of Darien." The center contained 95,180 square feet, covered 9.5

acres, and was anchored by a Grand Union supermarket. The New Jersey-based chain had recently passed through several hands and bankruptcies, and in 1998 was in the midst of what it hoped would be a turnaround. That was not to be, and the Grand Union at the Goodwives Shopping Plaza would ultimately be taken over by Shaw's.

Darien, with a population of about twenty thousand, is in Fairfield County, four miles from Stamford, in the heart of UBP's target zone for acquisitions. In 1998, the average cost of a new single-family house in the area was $575,000, a price that has since doubled. Favorable zoning laws will hold down local competition for the Goodwives center in the future.

In Greenwich, now UBP's headquarters, office space had become a premium. When a property at 25 Valley Drive, only about a mile from its headquarters, became available at an attractive price, UBP purchased the twenty-thousand-square-foot building.

In 1998, UBP advised shareholders regarding acquisition prospects: "We have targeted over 150 shopping centers in our market with a value of over $2 billion." But although the company suggested that "hard work" and "perseverance" would help the REIT convert a goodly number of those potentialities into actualities, prudence was also—and still is—a byword at Urstadt Biddle. The REIT business environment continued to be a bit tricky in 1999, with the NAREIT index that measured the financial health of REITs similar to UBP down by more than 10 percent. Prudence dictated that while the company needed to keep moving forward, it also needed to do so, as it always had, with small carefully chosen steps.

In the business atmosphere of the late 1990s, generally characterized by the tech stock driven, gyrating securities market, UBP continued to keep to the basics, with its eye more on Main Street than Wall Street. In fact, aside from the Arcadian Center acquisition, finalized early in the year, UBP added just one new shopping center in 1999, the Towne Centre in Somers, New York, where it already owned the Heritage 202 Center, adjacent to the new acquisition. Gristede's Supermarket anchored the shopping center. Founded in 1891 and incorporated as Gristede Brothers in 1913, the mostly Manhattan-centered Gristede's chain expanded into Westchester County and Connecticut in the 1920s. It had been combined with Sloan's chain of stores in 1997. Other tenants at Towne Centre included the financially stable Bank of New York, Astoria Federal Savings, and a US post office, all with long-term leases.

UBP used a tax-deferred exchange to effect the $9.5 million acquisition, its sixteenth since 1993. A major part of the purchase was financed by UBP's sale of Mervyns Department Store in Mesa, Arizona, thus trimming a noncore property from its portfolio while simultaneously adding a property in its acquisitions target area. With the completion of this transaction, Urstadt Biddle Properties had reduced its noncore properties to eight, one of which was a modest 4.2 acres of undeveloped land in Denver.

The Towne Centre, built in 1992 and located on 10.8 acres, contained almost seventy-eight thousand square feet of leasable space and a parking lot that could accommodate 410 cars. It bordered on Route 202. With the look of a "village square," the property, although relatively small, was also one of the most attractive in the UBP portfolio.

Meanwhile in 1999, UBP was growing by increasing the leased-up percentage of its available space to 96 percent, an improvement of 3 percent over the previous year. This activity included filling in a 115,000-square-foot vacancy at the Five Town Plaza in Springfield, Massachusetts, caused by the Caldor bankruptcy. Taking over the old Caldor space, and the new anchor of the shopping center, was Spag's Supply, Inc.

Spag's, a New England discount chain that began in 1934 in Shrewsbury, Massachusetts, might qualify as the tenant in the UBP portfolio with the most colorful history. Its name is said to have originated with the favorite dish of founder Anthony Borgatti: spaghetti. The iconoclastic Borgatti—subject of the book, *Spag: An American Business Legend*—favored a cowboy hat for headwear, and a cowboy hat became the company's logo. The chain's inventory had been nothing if not diverse, including over the years everything from pencils to cameras to nurses uniforms. Until a few years before it took space in the Five Town Plaza, Spag's adopted a policy that customers brought their own bags, hence the store's slogan, "No bags at Spag's."

Less colorful but just as important in 1999 was the continued upgrading of UBP's Carmel ShopRite Center, where Gold's Gym and a soon-to-open eight-plex cinema occupied thirty-five thousand square feet. Redevelopment had also paid off at the Ridgefield Center, where occupancy was now a healthy 95 percent.

While UBP's noncore properties were all ultimately scheduled to be sold, they too contributed to the company's bottom line. For example, at UBP's St. Louis distribution facility, the ten-year renewal lease to Chrysler for 170,000 square feet provided that the tenant, at its expense, would expand and renovate the facility, thereby adding value to the property.

The year 1999 also saw the retirement of James O. York from the company's board of directors. George J. Vojta, the CEO of the Westchester Group and a director of Private Export Funding Corporation and the New York State Banking Board, replaced him. Formerly vice chairman of Bankers Trust Company, Vojta—who was also a director of Globset, an Internet company serving financial institutions—possessed expertise that could prove especially useful as UBP approached the twenty-first century.

Internet shopping was just becoming a phenomenon to which UBP and other retail REITs had to pay heed. At the director's meeting on September 15, 1999, Urstadt and Biddle, according to the minutes of the meeting, "updated the Board on management's efforts to stay abreast of the threat of 'e-commerce' which offers consumers the availability of a wide variety of products for purchase via Internet access. In particular, Mr. Biddle described emerging efforts by some vendors to make groceries available through online purchasing." If the sound of a mouse clicking were to replace that of a cash register's ringing, there could be serious repercussions for companies whose bottom line depended on the success of brick-and-mortar stores, especially REITs whose shopping centers were usually anchored by supermarkets.

Indicative of the coming of a new age, the word "Internet" appeared in UBP's annual report for the first time in 1999. Noting the potential online competition, the report expressed confidence that "consumers will continue to visit our shopping centers to buy groceries, drop off their laundry, get a haircut, take home a pizza or run any one of a dozen chores they do every day."

In the bottom line of the final year of the old century, UBP showed total assets of about $184 million and just under $12 million funds from operations. The total cash dividend for common and Class A stock was $1.44, representing 63 percent of FFO.

Chapter Six

A NEW CENTURY

As the old century passed, every branch of the media was looking back and ahead to offer a picture of America on the cusp of... something. The Knight Ridder newswire's picture of real estate investment trusts on the eve of the millennium was a portrait in gray, at best:

> Considered the darlings of Wall Street two years ago, Real Estate Investment Trusts find themselves out of favor and growth-capital poor today.
>
> And as 1999 winds down, the publicly traded companies remain on the acquisition sidelines, their undervalued stocks vying for attention with the more provocative—and popular—dot-com and tech companies.

REITs may have been in the doldrums, at least as far as Wall Street was concerned, but UBP management paid little heed and kept going about its business. It saw the new millennium as offering new opportunities. In fact, the company's executives expressed their positive evaluation of UBP's own stock in the most dramatic way possible: they kept buying it.

Nevertheless, caution continued to be the byword at UBP at this time. In its annual report for 2000, management underlined the prevailing spirit of that year: "We do not believe in buying property simply to make a purchase." Thus 2000 did not see dramatic increases in the Urstadt Biddle portfolio. But in the background, the REIT was laying the foundation for the solid gains and considerable growth that would come in the years to follow.

Part of that foundation was making noncore properties more valuable, an essential part of the company's plan to dispose of these far-flung properties, but only under favorable conditions. That work paid off twice in the year as the company sold its noncore retail facilities leased to Value City Stores in Jonesboro,

Georgia, and to Navistar in Syracuse, New York. These transactions brought profits of $800,000 and $200,000, respectively.

Meanwhile, leasing—and UBP's leasing team under vice president for Leasing Linda Imhof—was in the spotlight in 2000. The company spent $6 million upgrading its facilities, and the results were clearly worth the investment. New tenants included Christmas Tree Shops at Danbury Square and Old Navy at Townline Square in Meriden. With the addition of the Cinema North Movie Theaters multiplex to its Carmel shopping center, UBP could now boast of the only movie theaters in Putnam County. Linens 'n Things also contracted for space that would soon become available at UBP's Newington, New Hampshire, location. The Christmas Tree Shops lease, in particular, required a good deal of finesse. As Willing Biddle wrote at the time, "We had to be creative in order to deliver the size store they needed. We had to relocate four tenants and buy out one, but the overall deal restored virtually all the 193,000 square feet available there to full occupancy, and we will have a vibrant center once again."

Specializing in giftware and housewares, Christmas Tree Shops had been founded in Massachusetts in 1970. It operated about thirty-five stores in New England and the Mid-Atlantic region and would be absorbed by Bed Bath & Beyond in 2003. Old Navy, specializing in value-priced clothing, was owned by the Gap, the more-than-three-thousand-store chain that also owned the more upscale Banana Republic group of clothing retailers. Linens 'n Things was a national chain headquartered in Clifton, New Jersey. It totaled about five hundred stores and featured brand-name housewares and home accessories.

Not only were new stores coming in at the shopping centers, but UBP was also developing vacant space, formerly occupied by a beer distribution center, for occupancy by Westchester Community College at the Arcadian Shopping Center. The college's Ossining Extension Center, specializing in biotechnology and healthcare, would locate there in 2001. The college described this facility as containing "fully equipped, state of the art science and health skills labs. In addition to courses in the life sciences, liberal arts and English as a Second Language, the center also offers professional development opportunities for those working in the health care field." According to *Real Estate Weekly*, "the college signed a 10-year lease and occupies 12,500 SF of space in a commercial building acquired by UBP in 1999. The Company recently completed a $1.5 million renovation to prepare the facility for use by the college." Biotechnology was a growth area in Westchester County, and the college aimed to use its new facility to train future employees—eight thousand were already employed in the industry in the county—in that field.

As Willing Biddle was to sum it up in an article he wrote for *Real Estate Weekly* in March 2001, "This is hardly a traditional tenant, but the chances are the County of Westchester is not going to be subject to every change in the wind that buffets dot-coms and discount stores, and we know that a few thousand students coming and going each week will help our retailers."

New leases and lease renewals, in fact, accounted for 732,000 square feet of space in fiscal 2000, 20 percent of the leasable area in UBP's core property. Overall, UBP was 97 percent leased, an increase of 1 percent over the previous year. According to UBP president Willing Biddle, it was "one of our best leasing years."

These accomplishments were especially impressive because they came during a year when three major tenants at UBP's Danbury Square Shopping Center failed, reducing the company's income by $600,000 compared to the previous year. The bankruptcy of large retail chains had become a serious problem for all retail REITs; and in the previous five years, more than a dozen, representing four hundred thousand square feet of space, had gone under in UBP shopping centers. At the board meeting on December 13, 2000, Chairman Urstadt noted "that management was studying defenses to the Company's heavy retail exposure." One approach receiving serious consideration, but later abandoned, would have been to take advantage of what was proving to be a growth field with enormous potential: leasing medical office space.

UBP, always with an eye to the future, at this time also boosted its bank credit line, strengthening its "war chest" so as to be prepared to take advantage of value when management spotted it. The prospect for raising any future capital that the company might need had also brightened. Credit rating agency Fitch Duff & Phelps took another look at UBP and upped its preferred stock rating from BB — to BB, the only REIT upgraded by that agency in that year. UBP CFO James Moore pointed out that mortgages, at 30 percent of the company's total capitalization, was "conservative given the current economic climate."

Considering the hit UBP took from three bankruptcies, the slight up tick in its FFO for 2000—the seventh consecutive annual increase, averaging 8 percent a year over that span—had to be considered a positive sign. Total annual dividends for both classes of common stock, up again in 2000, were approaching $1.50, representing a 10 percent yield per share. And still the payout as a percentage of FFO had been kept to a low 65 percent, a conservative figure compared to that of similar REITs, enabling UBP to reward shareholders with steady dividends while at the same time priming itself for further investment and growth. With these figures, the company could truthfully assert in its annual report that Urstadt Biddle was still "undervalued and overlooked."

A Year to Remember

The following year, 2001, could perhaps best be characterized, in the manner of Charles Dickens, as the best of times and the worst of times.

Obviously, any business has to be prepared for all sorts of contingencies; but nobody could have anticipated the business environment, fortunately brief, that was created by the events of September 11, 2001. As fate would have it, UBP Chairman Charles Urstadt was at a meeting at the World Financial Center, across the street from the World Trade Center, on September 10, the day before the terrorists struck. The center sustained serious damage when the Twin Towers collapsed.

Fortunately, nobody from the UBP family was lost or injured in the attack, nor were any of its facilities or tenants damaged. Since the company's core locations were all in the suburbs of New York City or beyond, the curtailment of transportation in the metropolitan area that went on for about a week did not have any direct effect on patrons or tenants of UBP's shopping centers; nor did it hamper operations at the company headquarters in Greenwich, also well into the suburbs. (Although the parking lot at the Wayne, New Jersey, shopping center would, for a while, overflow with cars left by commuters who were suddenly forced onto public transportation, preventing some shopping center patrons from finding parking spaces.) Since most of the company's centers were anchored by supermarkets and concentrated on merchandise and services that people needed under any circumstance, sales were not significantly impaired. That orientation toward the basics had been built into UBP strategy with economic cycles in mind, but here it also proved beneficial in the face of a kind of economic uncertainty that no one could have imagined. There were probably many people involved in the hotel sector of the REIT industry, hard hit by 9/11, who wished they could have been saying the same thing.

In fact, as UBP president Willing Biddle explained to the *Westchester County Business Journal* in November, "While attendance at shopping malls has been down during the month of September, surveys showed that grocery and personal care products enjoyed increased sales. People are staying closer to home and shopping locally which helps our tenants who include Stop and Shop, ShopRite, A&P, Gristede's and Shaws."

Nevertheless, the company would feel a few ripples from the shock of that day, and one of them was personal. By 2001, the company had made great strides in its announced strategic plan to reposition its real estate portfolio and concentrate in the northeast. It had been successful to this point in selling off much of its noncore assets, modestly adding mortgage debt to its strong balance sheet and selling equity in a successful private placement of Class A common stock in 1998.

It was now time to re-enter the capital markets and raise equity in a public stock offering. UBP hired Ferris, Baker Watts (FBW) and its REIT banking group, headed by Mark Decker and his son Mark, Jr., to advise the company on a public stock sale. UBP hadn't entered the public markets since 1980, but the recent debacle in the dot-com and tech stock industries had soured investors on that sector, and they had an increased interest in a real product with real earnings and the ability to generate cash. That made REITs look very attractive.

Mark Decker organized the project and added Hilliard Lyons and Morgan Keegan to the underwriting group. The attacks of 9/11 had closed the capital markets for days afterward, with trading suspended, just as the project was getting underway. Nevertheless, determined to go forward with the stock offering, a management team comprised of Charles Urstadt, Wing Biddle, and Jim Moore embarked on a whirlwind tour of brokerage offices around the country to market the company and its stock offering to the various retail stockbrokers at FBW, Hilliard Lyons, and Morgan Keegan in what is commonly referred to as a "road show."

The first leg of the road show would take Urstadt, Biddle, and Moore to Washington DC, where FBW is headquartered. The team arranged a flight out of LaGuardia Airport in New York and would land at Reagan National Airport in Washington DC. Air traffic had only recently been reopened in the country, and this day would be the first time that flights to the Washington DC area would be permitted. Airport security was extremely tight. Passengers were randomly selected for physical inspection and a hand-baggage check. At that time, air marshals, inconspicuous in plain clothes, were on all flights to the DC area. As the UBP team entered the plane, an announcement to the passengers came over the intercom: "Please take your seats. Once you have taken your seat, please do not leave your seat for any reason while the plane is airborne."

About halfway through the normally one-hour flight, the attendant came by offering refreshments. Urstadt, Biddle, and Moore all asked for Cokes. Suddenly, as the attendant handed Jim Moore his drink, the cup slipped from his hand and spilled onto his lap. He instinctively leaped to his feet to minimize the damage. As he did, two air marshals also jumped from their seats, identifying themselves and preparing to take out this potential "terrorist" before he could threaten the aircraft and its passengers. Quickly the attendant reacted: "It's only a can of Coke!"

An embarrassed Jim Moore quickly sat down, his lap soaking, and stayed that way for the remainder of the trip. But there was one more shock to come. The team arrived at its Washington DC hotel to find it surrounded by SWAT teams. Could this possibly be related to the "Coke caper" on the plane? Hardly. As fate would have it, a convention of 1,500 Muslims was taking place at the hotel!

By spring 2002, it would be clear that the 9/11 attack was contributing to an increase in the cost of insurance. At the board of director's meeting held on June 12, 2002, the subject of "terrorism insurance" was raised. On March 12, 2003, Ray Argila, head of the Law Department, reported to the board that the company was implementing a "disaster recovery" program in which all essential company documents were being scanned onto discs, which were being stored off-site. A positive side effect of that program was that some documents that had previously not been digitized were now made accessible by computer in the company's database, adding to UBP's efficiency.

The cover of the 2001 annual report reflected the patriotic fervor engendered in the country by the sneak attack of 9/11. A bar chart whose red, white, and blue colors and star motif, not to mention the American flag flying from the top of the last and highest bar, clearly stated the company's feelings about what happened that day. UBP also manifested another popular response to 9/11: The country and its economy will not only not be beaten down but will continue to grow and prosper. The chart shows increases in dividends, funds from operations, and revenue. Below the chart, UBP stated: "We are the Right company. In the Right business. In the Right place. At the Right time." Each repetition of the word "right" is printed in red.

In April, the journal *Financial Planning* commented: "Investors who've abandoned the tech sector in favor of something more stable may find what they're looking for in real estate investment trusts." They did, indeed, find that stability, especially in one REIT. Wall Street finally noticed that the Greenwich, Connecticut, REIT it had been overlooking had been steadily building value all along while the tech stock fad had inevitably run its course. When 9/11 further shook investor faith in all but the most solid performers, "meat and potatoes" never looked so good!

The year's numbers for UBP tell the dramatic story. For the calendar year 2001, total return to UBP stockholders—dividends plus the growth in the value of the company's stock—measured 63.9 percent for its common stock. By comparison, similar figures for NAREIT's shopping center sector registered 29.9 percent, 13.9 percent for the NAREIT Equity index as a whole, 11.5 percent for the S&P, and 5.4 percent for the Dow Jones Average. As the company summed it up at year's end: "2001 marked a turning point in which perception came close to the reality of performance." The image of UBP on Wall Street was finally beginning to resemble the way it looked to the REIT's management on Railroad Avenue in Greenwich.

When it came to dividend consistency, it was an old story retold. UBP declared its 129th quarterly dividend at $0.72 per common share and $0.80 for each Class A common share. Total dividends constituted 65 percent of FFO.

The 4.8 million shares of Class A common stock that UBP sold in October went out at $9.30 per share and were augmented by the almost seven hundred thousand shares the underwriters—Ferris, Baker Watts, Inc.; Hilliard Lyons, Inc.; and Advest, Inc.—bought under their option a month later. The net result was $47 million that UBP could apply to new acquisitions. To go along with and enhance those numbers, mortgages made up only 25 percent of Urstadt Biddle's capitalization.

UBP was looking good on all fronts. The occupancy rate in UBP's portfolio hit 98 percent, with staggered leases helping to hold down turnovers in any one year. Among its tenants, none represented more than 6 percent of the company's revenue, a far cry from the precarious exposure of HREI years before to reliance on the fortunes of only a few tenants. Funds from operations, the truest measure of how the company was faring, was up for a very satisfying eighth straight year, with an annual growth rate averaging 8 percent in that period. The previous year it had been $11.9 million. In 2001, FFO was $14.6 million, mainly the result of some choice acquisitions and effective leasing.

In 2001, Urstadt Biddle continued to aggressively pursue appropriate acquisitions in its target area. In an article written by CEO Charles Urstadt that appeared in *Real Estate Weekly* on September 12, 2001 (the date might have qualified it for the headline, "It Was The Best Of Times; It Was The Worst Of Times"), Urstadt identified his company's strategy in the context of changing times: "We're local guys. I've lived in Westchester for 60 years—and we know the region and its impressive demographics well . . . . The Internet may yet prove to be a good way to buy and sell, but people like to go out to the store to buy their groceries. Through boom and bust, this is a good place to build a sound retail-based real estate business."

Putting that strategy into practice, the featured acquisition in 2001 was the purchase in August of the Chilmark Shopping Center in Briarcliff Manor, New York, which was less than two miles from UBP's Arcadian Center. The purchase, at a cost of $7.1 million, came via a tax deferred reverse exchange of real estate. The thirty-eight-thousand-square-foot shopping center, located on 4.3 acres, was 93 percent leased. Chilmark came with eighteen tenants, including such brand-name stores as RadioShack, the renowned national chain of stores featuring small consumer electronics and related accessories, and the Dress Barn, which had originated in Stamford in 1962 and now had about eight hundred stores nationwide.

Briarcliff Manor, fifteen minutes northwest of White Plains, with a median family income of just under $160,000 a year at the time UBP made this purchase, boasted one of the best school districts in America and was also the location of a major branch campus of Pace University. Chilmark, named for an old mansion in the area, was the name of the neighborhood in which the shopping center was located.

In another smaller acquisition, Urstadt Biddle, following a strategy of "acquiring high yield office properties near our executive office in Greenwich, Connecticut," as its annual report phrased it, purchased a medical office building at 7 Riversville Road in Greenwich. This acquisition also had the additional benefit of adding some diversity to the company's portfolio in the increasingly important medical services area.

One thing fortunately missing in 2001 was a factor in UBP's success that year: vacancies. It was another good year for leasing, and the company-wide vacancy rate had shrunk to 2 percent. Between new and renewed leases, 14 percent of UBP's leasable space, a total of 352,000 square feet, was contracted for in 2001. Leasing activity was especially prominent at the Townline Square Center in Meriden, where the company signed new leases with retailing giants Burlington Coat Factory, Old Navy, and Linens 'n Things. The leasing activity at Townline was encouraging because it greatly approved the attractiveness of the center for its other retail tenants. As UBP president Willing Biddle commented: "The addition of Old Navy and Linens 'N Things now resolves a long time leasing problem at the center created when The Wiz vacated the Center in 1998. We anticipate that these prestigious retailers will benefit all of the current tenants in the 300,000 square foot shopping center and will enable our leasing team to complete the retenanting of the balance of the property this year."

In Tempe, Arizona, where its shopping center, although outside of the company's target area was still profitable, UBP enhanced its value with a new ten-year lease with a branch of the 99 Cents Only stores. The popular off-price chain took thirty-one thousand square feet in a lease valued at about $1.6 million. UBP also signed a new lease, which included a rent increase, with Giffels Associates at its Southfield, Michigan, office building covering one hundred thousand square feet. The lease's value was about $14 million.

Even the bankruptcy of Grand Union, the anchor supermarket tenant at the Goodwives Shopping Center in Darien, didn't cause UBP to skip a beat. In fact, it actually turned out to be a net gain for the company. UBP's leasing team convinced Shaw's Supermarkets, the prominent New England chain, to buy the lease and do an eight-thousand-square-foot expansion at the location.

Finally, Kimco, which had been both adversary and partner to the REIT that became Urstadt Biddle Properties, was taken out of the picture when UBP sold its share in its joint venture with Kimco, the 231,000-square-foot Countryside Square Village Shopping Center in Clearwater, Florida. The company, following its strategy of disposing of noncore properties, also sold its warehouse in Albany, Georgia, and the undeveloped land it owned in Denver.

As 2001 ended, as the result of a liquidity crunch felt by the holder of two hundred thousand shares of the company's Series B preferred stock, UBP was able to repurchase these shares at a discount to par for just over $16 million. The transaction represented an increase in shareholder equity of about $3 million.

Coping with Sarbanes-Oxley

If much of the story of 2001 concerned maintaining stability and growth in the shadow of the attack on the World Trade Center and the economic uncertainties that followed, 2002 saw a different kind of shadow begin to darken the business environment, not only for Urstadt Biddle Properties but also for many other small cap REITs. In response to widely publicized corporate governance and accounting scandals centered on a few firms, including Enron and WorldCom, Congress in 2002 passed the legislation known as the Sarbanes-Oxley Act. Intended to tighten corporate governance and accounting procedures, the legislation was viewed by many business people as having gone too far, imposing onerous, debilitating, and often unnecessary rules and regulations on companies that would substantially and unfairly raise the cost of doing business. Interviewed at a NAREIT forum in June, Willing Biddle told a reporter, "It has been a considerable burden on us."

In the process of complying with all of the new regulations, Urstadt Biddle found it necessary to replace its longtime auditor, Arthur Andersen, which was indicted in the spring of 2002 for its role in the Enron scandal, with Ernst & Young. The transition went smoothly. But the cost of the auditing services provided, which soon reached $975 an hour per partner, were becoming a serious concern.

At the end of 2003, UBP had to devote valuable time to drawing up a formal code of ethics and a "whistle blower" policy to meet the requirements of the Securities and Exchange Commission and the New York Stock Exchange, both of which were responding to the new, cautious environment. These documents formally spelled out rules for avoiding conflict of interest, insider trading, and the use of the Internet and e-mail. A mere glance at the company's board of directors meeting minutes and other office records clearly demonstrates how the paperwork was piling up to meet the new regulations.

The concerns raised by the Sarbanes-Oxley Act would continue to preoccupy management at Urstadt Biddle, as they would many other firms. Estimates of the "hit" that REITs would take from Sarbanes-Oxley ranged from two to five cents a share, and there was widespread concern that the burdens of staying "public" would push many firms into going private. At the end of 2003, Matt Valley, the editor of *National Real Estate Investor* commented: "Only a few years ago, the mere mention of 'corporate governance' was enough to put anyone to sleep. No hard-charging, cutting-edge corporate executive had time to be overly preoccupied with audit committee meetings, right? How times have changed as illustrated by the ongoing corporate scandals on Wall Street, which continue to ooze like a never-ending tube of toothpaste. In today's climate, a panel discussion on the Sarbanes-Oxley Act—which regulates the accounting industry and seeks to improve the disclosure practices of public companies—is virtually guaranteed to fill a room." Feelings about the act and the need to modify it still continue to run strong. For some, these new forms of overhead could constitute a cure that could also kill.

The Goodwives Shopping Plaza, in affluent Darien Connecticut, which Urstadt Biddle added to its portfolio in 1998, contains 95,180 sq ft., covers 9.5 acres, and is anchored by a Shaws supermarket.

The Arcadian Shopping Center in the Briarcliff Manor/Ossining area in Westchester County, New York, was a 1998 acquisition.

A block of stores, offices and a few apartments in the heart of downtown Ridgefield, Connecticut. Although not a shopping center like most of the other Urstadt Biddle Properties, the purchase was a good one because the area had seen significant growth and building over the past three decades.

The Chilmark Shopping Center in Briarcliff Manor, New York, less than two miles from UBP's Arcadian Center, was a 2001 acquisition.

Urstadt Biddle Properties board of directors in December 2007: Top row, left to right: Willing L. Biddle, George J. Vojta, Robert J. Mueller, Charles D. Urstadt. Bottom row, left to right: George H.C. Lawrence, E. Virgil Conway, Charles J. Urstadt, Robert R. Douglass, Peter Herrick.

In 2002, the Ridgeway Shopping Center in Stamford, Connecticut represented UBP's largest acquisition ever, bringing in 360,000 square feet of leaseable space, including 29,000 square feet of office space.

Unprecedented Prosperity

There was little that Urstadt Biddle could do to bring about the needed reform of Sarbanes-Oxley, other than continue to work with other REITs through NAREIT to modify the legislation. Fortunately UBP's future success was largely in its own hands. And at the beginning of 2002, the company strengthened its position for future growth with the naming of James Aries as vice president, Acquisitions and Leasing. Most recently director of Leasing at Kin Properties, White Plains, New York, Aries had previously served as vice president for Leasing at Bryant Development, Purchase, New York, and director of real estate at Melville Corp., Rye, New York. Aries came from a Westchester family whose experience in real estate dated back about a century.

Aries joined Urstadt Biddle just in time to be part of the company's greatest growth spurt in its history. UBP would characterize 2002 in its annual report as a "great year," and in no small way that was due to its acquisition that year of four shopping centers, three of them in Connecticut's affluent Fairfield County and the other in New York's similarly affluent Westchester County. All told, these additions to the UBP portfolio occurred within a fifteen-month span that saw the company acquire properties for which it expended $150 million.

The first acquisition of 2002 was a modest one: the thirty-three-thousand-square-foot, 2.7-acre Airport Plaza Shopping Center in Danbury, Connecticut, located across the road from the Danbury Square property that UBP already owned, and the enormous Danbury Fair Mall. The company bought the Danbury property in March, which was 100 percent leased with tenants including Sleepy's and FuncoLand, for about $7 million.

And Urstadt Biddle was only warming up. In July, the company acquired the Ridgeway Shopping Center in Stamford, Connecticut, from a partnership partly controlled by Larry Silverstein, the developer who owned the World Trade Center. More than ten times the size of UBP's previous purchase of the Airport Plaza Shopping Center, Ridgeway represented UBP's largest acquisition ever and brought in 360,000 square feet of leasable space, including 29,000 square feet of office space. Fairfield County's largest open-air shopping center, Ridgeway cost the company just under $90 million. A Stop & Shop Supermarket covered 60,000 square feet of that space and anchored the center. Altogether there were thirty-five tenants, among them Bed Bath & Beyond, Marshals, Old Navy, and Staples. Michaels Crafts, another of the national chains at Ridgeway, was the biggest purveyor of arts and crafts supplies in America. Originating in Texas, the eight-hundred-store chain featured about forty thousand items at each location.

The Ridgeway Shopping Center was emblematic of the transformation that retailing had gone through in the country since World War II. Constructed in the 1950s during the migration to the suburbs and the rise of the automobile to a central position in the way that Americans shopped, the center had undergone extensive renovation and expansion over the past decade to accommodate the big-box stores of the modern shopping era. The retail portion was 96 percent leased, but there was over thirty thousand square feet of vacant space; and UBP intended to undertake further renovation work to insure that it would be fully leased and be competitive with the new Waterfront Shopping Center, then under development in Port Chester, to the south of Stamford and within shopping distance of Greenwich as well.

The Ridgeway Center was midway between the Merritt Parkway and I-95, the Connecticut Turnpike, and bordered by two of Stamford's major traffic arteries. "Ridgeway enjoys a unique position in the market being at the northern edge of Stamford's downtown," company president Willing Biddle remarked about the purchase. "The Center benefits from both a transient office worker population and the densely populated Stamford residential neighborhoods surrounding the property." He characterized Ridgeway as "one of the premier shopping centers in the state of Connecticut." It was, to put it simply, the most significant retail acquisition in the company's history.

Not that the company was going to rest on its 2002 laurels. By 2003, UBP would already be in the midst of a substantial upgrade of the Ridgeway Center, replacing an old movie theater, shuttered since 2000, and the thirty thousand square feet of vacant office space with a $5 million renovation—the cost of which was shared by the new tenant, an LA Fitness Sports Clubs facility. The newly adapted space of almost fifty thousand square feet featured a seventy-five-foot-long, five-lane swimming pool. Alert Urstadt Biddle employees may have caught the extra enthusiasm that company chairman Charles Urstadt displayed when he spoke of this facility since Urstadt, in his seventies, was himself a former world champion and still a national champion swimmer, holding five national records for the fifty-meter breaststroke in the seventy-five to seventy-nine age group. Urstadt would go on to garner several gold medals at the 2007 New York State Empire Games. For Urstadt, competitive swimming was "a question of goals and achievement. Not unlike in the real estate business, there is a satisfaction of achieving the goals I set for myself with these competitions." Unfortunately, zoning and construction complications would keep him from taking his first dip in this new pool until the summer of 2006.

Health clubs were definitely part of a growth industry. There had been 6,211 in existence in 1982, but by the time UBP was readying space for this latest facility, the number had grown to more than twenty thousand. In the past year alone, membership in health clubs had grown by 3 million nationally. In fact, the 3,500 members that LA Fitness had planned for turned out to be seven thousand.

The two shopping centers Urstadt Biddle had purchased by midyear would alone have made 2002 a good year. What made it "great" was the announcement the company had in store for Christmas Eve. In late December (officially, the company closed on the properties in early January 2003), UBP announced the addition of not one but two more centers to its portfolio. They were the seventy-eight-thousand-square-foot Orange Meadows Shopping Center in Orange, Connecticut, conveniently and profitably located in the Route 1 corridor, and the Westchester Pavilion Shopping Center in the heart of downtown White Plains, an area that had seen enormous growth and construction in the past decade.

The seven-acre Orange Meadow facility, which cost UBP about $11 million, was 85 percent leased, thus posing both a challenge and opportunity to UBP to upgrade and fill the empty space with quality tenants at favorable rents, further increasing the value of the property. Stores already on board included Seaman's Furniture, Thomasville Furniture, and a Talbot's clothing store. Trader Joe's anchored Orange Meadow. This specialty gourmet supermarket—everything from a mini quiche to canned turkey chili—was known for holding down costs by selling its own brand of prepared foods. Trader Joe's was also into the hip ethos of its young and affluent customers. How many other supermarkets brag that their products "rock"? Of those products, perhaps none "rocked" more, or gained more publicity, than vintner Charles Shaw's $1.99 bottle of wine. Affectionately known as "Two-Buck Chuck," it had become something of a national institution and had forced many large liquor retailers to compete by finding similar bargain bottles to offer their customers.

But the big package under the tree on December 24 was the 185,000-square-foot, fourteen-acre Westchester Pavilion Shopping Center, which UBP acquired for just under $40 million in cash from the State of Wisconsin Retirement Fund, which had held the property since 1994. In the 1950s, the site on which the center stood had been an Alexander's Department Store that had closed in 1988. In the mid-1990s the department store was replaced by the three-story Pavilion, which adjoined the 828,000-square-foot slightly more upscale Westchester Mall, anchored by Neiman Marcus and Nordstrom department stores and the Crowne Plaza Hotel. And a new Fortunoff's was in the works just down the street.

"We look for a certain return on investment," Urstadt Biddle CFO James R. Moore told the *Westchester County Business Journal*. "In the case of the Westchester Pavilion, it is a quality property and it happened to be offered by a broker. The seller, which is a public institution, wanted the property sold by the end of the year and we were able to make that happen." Expanding on UBP's meat-and-potatoes orientation, Moore added that "the type of properties we buy—the basic necessities-type shopping center is our bread and butter property—are sort of recession proof, which makes us a retail sharpshooter."

The neighborhood in White Plains surrounding UBP's new shopping center was a dynamic one. As the *New York Times* would write in 2005: "In the rejuvenated climate that is this city's attraction to developers and businesses, with towers going up and new stores moving in fast, empty space in most malls doesn't stand vacant for long."

The nearby Galleria Shopping Center was also in the process of being sold, and also in the area was the City Center at White Plains, a $320 million project involving five hundred thousand square feet of space that would include six hundred apartments. Said John Merrit, UBP VP for Acquisitions, "We love what's happening in White Plains. It's great to see it awaken after years of languishing. The residential elements that are being introduced will just round out the city. More residents mean more shoppers."

In something of a departure for UBP, its new eight-tenant center was a vertical-enclosed mall instead of the older, more traditional street-level center. In addition, it offered room for expansion, since the three-floor total was one short of the four levels that the city had originally approved for the site in 1991. The pavilion was 99 percent leased and among its tenants were Borders Books and Records, Educational Warehouse, Toys"R"Us, OfficeMax, Sports Authority, Outback Steakhouse, and McDonald's. Several of the stores in the mall ranked among the top ten performers in their chain in sales per square foot, an indication of just how hot the Westchester, and especially the White Plains area, had become at the time of the UBP purchase.

Several of the tenants at the pavilion offered prime examples of where retail trends were heading. The Sports Authority, for example, which occupied forty-three thousand square feet, had begun with one store in Florida in 1987. By 2002, it boasted about two hundred stores across America. Purchased by Kmart and then spun off, the chain kept growing, keying into America's interest in athletics and fitness. A year after UBP bought the pavilion, Sports Authority would merge with Gart Sports to become the largest sporting goods chain in the country.

Outback Steakhouse, begun just a year after the Sports Authority in 1988, was a place where a family could eat out even in a recession. In 2007 a 14-ounce New York strip steak was still priced under $20. The hook at this popular eatery—part of an international chain—was a little Aussie chic, suggestive of the active, informal life Down Under, where friendliness means tossing another piece of steak or shrimp on the "barbie." Diners had come to expect the likes of stuffed crocodiles and boomerangs at Outback. The growth and popularity of the Outback chain paralleled the enormous and growing popularity of good, inexpensive Australian wines during this period. In fact, the ubiquitous Yellow Tail brand of Australian wines, featuring the Shiraz grape, was on the menu.

The Westchester Pavilion also offers a prime example of how astute management can maximize the return on a company's investments. Across the street from the shopping center's garage, a restaurant was cleverly advising its patrons that they could obtain "free parking" at the Pavilion while they dined off the center's premises. UBP quickly plugged the hole by charging for that parking, grossing $800,000 the first year.

While acquisitions held the spotlight in 2002, leasing was also holding up well. New and renewed leases accounted for 226,000 square feet of space, about a tenth of the total UBP inventory. Only a major vacancy at the office building in Southfield, Michigan, where a downsizing tenant left more than 60,000 square feet empty, kept the occupancy rate from equaling the previous year's 98 percent. The recently purchased Ridgeway Center, which had 40,000 square feet vacant, also skewed the results. Even 95 percent occupancy was good, and there was opportunity to increase cash flow through more leasing. Among the year's highlights: another Outback Steakhouse took space at Newington Park, and UBP completed the retenanting of Townline Square.

The numbers tell in an even simpler way why 2002 was "great" for Urstadt Biddle. Net income was up 53 percent on total revenues that advanced 23 percent. The company was now also bigger, as total assets increased by 62 percent. For stockholders, that added up to a 74 percent increase in equity. Needless to say, with these kinds of figures, dividends were up for a ninth consecutive year. In fact, the total return on the Company's Class A common stock was about three times that of the NAREIT All REIT index; and that, in turn, was during a period in which the economy was hardly flourishing.

Even the slight decrease in funds from operations per share came about from something that was good for the company. UBP issued $13 million in new Class A shares. The money thus raised was temporarily parked in low-yield investments so as to have capital readily accessible for new acquisitions. This diluted FFO per share. Actual FFO, however, increased from $14.6 to $21 million.

All in all, Chairman Urstadt declared in December, fiscal 2002 was "probably the Company's best year ever, evidenced in part by the Company's growth in revenues and nearly doubling its asset size."

As befitting a REIT named by Fortune's *Small Business Magazine* in 2003 as one of the one hundred fastest-growing small companies in America, Urstadt Biddle Properties continued its upward march that year on virtually every kind of chart one could devise to measure the economic health and progress of a business.

For the tenth year in a row—an old, but sweet song—dividends were up. Also up were funds from operations, gross revenues, and earnings.

Urstadt Biddle's acquisition rate had to slow a bit in 2003, but the company still kept growing. Acting as something of a brake was the seller's market created by lower interest rates and companies flush with cash to spend on new acquisitions. That meant competition for most worthwhile properties and the need to carefully measure potential purchase prices against potential value. As the company stressed in its 2003 annual report, "Size is vanity but profits are sanity." UBP would continue its tradition of growing only when growth made sense.

Nevertheless, even in this competitive environment, UBP wasn't going to completely stand still. Its May 29 sale of Series C senior cumulative preferred stock that added $40 million to Urstadt Biddle's funds set aside for acquisitions guaranteed that when management spotted an opportunity, the cash would be there to close on it.

Hardly had the ink dried on the documents transferring the two Christmas Eve purchases when UBP was back in the market for another shopping center. Only two months into 2003, UBP added the 100 percent-leased Green Farms Plaza Shopping Center in Westport, Connecticut, to its portfolio in a transaction that had been in the works since September. This forty-thousand-square-foot property on three acres was—like the Orange Meadows Center, which had been acquired in 2002—located in the busy Route 1 corridor.

Among the nine tenants in Green Farms Plaza was Pier One Imports, a home furnishings and decor retailer that had in a few short years become widely popular. Pier One accounted for 36 percent of the leasable space in the center. From its first store in San Mateo, California, opened in 1962, Pier One had grown into a chain of about 1,200 outlets across the country accounting for approximately $1.5 billion in sales. The stores carried everything from candles to upholstered furniture.

June 2003 saw Urstadt Biddle vary its acquisition profile slightly with the purchase of 126,000 square feet of space contained in the Somers Commons in Somers, New York, where it already owned two shopping centers. The acquired space consisted of seven condominium retail units out of the nine total at Somers Commons, costing the company $21.65 million in cash made available from the stock sale it had conducted less than one month prior to this purchase. The space occupied by UBP in the shopping center was a bit more than half of the Commons's total of 207,000 square feet. Serving the function of anchor tenant was a 72,000-square-foot Stop & Shop Supermarket, which was not part of the UBP purchase.

UBP president Willing Biddle, explaining the company's rationale for continuing to acquire property in Somers, told the *Fairfield County Business Journal* that UBP expected the Somers area to "continue to grow faster than southern Westchester." The annual average household income in Somers in 2000 was $107, 904, compared with the $99,465 countywide. The population of the area had also continued to grow; but the local government's slow growth policy, discussed earlier, had held down available shopping, making existing retail units that more valuable.

The new property was 95 percent leased. Tenants included Chili's Restaurant, Home Goods, Futurama Furniture, and RadioShack. Much of the space in the shopping center had been vacant until retenanting under a condominium arrangement introduced in 2002.

At the Arcadian Center in Ossining, which the company viewed as "an under managed property that we could renovate and improve" when it made the purchase, as Willing Biddle explained to a *New York Times* reporter, UBP had spent about $1 million on renovations. In 2003, a branch of Washington Mutual replaced a Bagel Emporium and Starbucks opened one of its ubiquitous facilities. The Washington Mutual branch replaced a portion of the space leased to Dress Barn, which that retailer consolidated into other space it occupied at Arcadian. For UBP, the switch was a net plus. As Willing Biddle put it, "This adds another service we didn't have. We want to have one of everything."

More and more, it was national chains with bigger budgets than were available to the more traditional smaller tenants that were taking space in shopping centers. The new tenants could afford to pay higher rents. Another advantage to having these kinds of tenants was that bank financing, if necessary at some point, was likely to be more forthcoming with such a prestigious tenant roster.

In its core properties in 2003, UBP maintained a 97 percent occupancy rate. Burlington Coat Factory and World Gym, added to the Five Town Plaza, immediately prospered. With only about 5 percent of its leased space in the core area up for renewal in the next two years, leasing was in very good shape. The $4 million that UBP allocated for improving its properties in 2004 further guaranteed that this segment of the company's performance would continue to be strong. The only weak spot was Southfield, Michigan, where the company's office building still had a good deal of vacant space in a weak office market.

Effective management of its properties had become as much a hallmark of UBP as was the steady and careful growth of its portfolio. Toward this end, the company added something new in 2003: the Segway Human Transporter. Maintaining security over the considerable square footage of a shopping center can be a big expense. Putting the security force on wheels at a reasonable price was a good way to meet this challenge, reducing by at least 50 percent the amount of time it took to inspect an entire shopping center. The Segway was a two-wheel, self-balancing scooter, capable of speeds up to about 12 miles per hour, that the company began testing at a few of its bigger centers, including the recently purchased Westchester Pavilion.

On May 1, 2003, Urstadt Biddle changed the stock ticker symbol of its Class A common stock from "UBP.A" to "UBA." "We expect that the change to 'UBA' will make it easier for our shareholders and their brokers to find us on a variety of information systems presently used in the stock brokerage industry," explained CEO Charles Urstadt. "Different services have identified the Class A Common stock, which is our most commonly traded equity security, variously as UBP.A, UBP/A, UBP'A, UBP-A, UBP A and UBPA which we believe confuses investors.

Furthermore, the four letter identifier has caused some investors to confuse the security with preferred stock. We believe it will be easier for the information services and our shareholders to locate and monitor our Class A Common shares when they begin trading under the three letter ticker symbol 'UBA'."

There were still other positive changes. On October 1, Urstadt Biddle Properties made it into the Standard & Poor's REIT Composite index. Ironically, the slot in the index had opened up because UBP's one-time nemesis, Kimco, had purchased Mid-Atlantic Realty Trust, the REIT that had previously occupied it. Also in 2003, Urstadt Biddle Properties added to its board of directors Robert J. Mueller, formerly a senior executive vice president of the Bank of New York and member of the bank's Senior Planning Committee. Not surprisingly, one of Mr. Mueller's areas of expertise at the bank was in commercial real estate lending.

A Bell Ringer—and Then Some

If 2002 was a "great" year for Urstadt Biddle and 2003 was, if anything, even better, what should be said about 2004? One is reminded of the snappy utterance so often associated with singer Frank Sinatra: "Ring-a-ding-ding!" To cap the year's achievements, on the afternoon of December 15, 2004, UBP's top management, along with its board of directors, gathered above the trading floor at the New York Stock Exchange to ring the closing bell for the day's trading. A photograph of the occasion in the 2004 annual report depicted smiles all around, with company president Willing Biddle standing in the middle and chairman Charles J. Urstadt, wearing a Kelly green tie and standing next to his son, Charles, proudly wielding the gavel to ring the bell.

There was a lot to smile about. In its thirty-fifth year as a publicly traded company and in Urstadt's thirtieth year as a member of the board and his fifteenth as chairman, even Wall Street was finally becoming aware that UBP was something special among REITs. In its eleventh year of steadily increasing dividends, Urstadt Biddle could now point to a new, steadily increasing number: the fourth straight year that the price of the company's stock had increased. Compared with the previous year, total revenues were up, as were net income and that all-important funds from operations.

Nevertheless, dividends still took pride of place at UBP, and the company kept churning them out every quarter with shareholder-pleasing regularity, as it had without missing even one for thirty-five years. Total annual dividends per share were up over the previous year.

UBP's operations during 2004 epitomized the reasons for that steady dividend. The company kept to its acquisitions game plan, staying focused on its core area, seeking out value-priced, supermarket-anchored shopping centers that—with the application of Urstadt Biddle's know-how in upgrading, retenanting, and managing—would bring a solid return on its investment.

With low interest rates encouraging property owners to refinance rather than sell and prices bid up because of stiff competition, only one shopping center met all of the company's criteria in 2004. Late in the year, after a long negotiation period, UBP purchased the Dock in Stratford, Connecticut, for $50 million, with the actual closing not coming until January 7, 2005. The Dock was the company's most notorious closing. The process started at 11:00 AM and ended at 7:30 AM the following day.

The timing of the purchase worked like a charm for Urstadt Biddle because an unsolicited offer to buy the Bi-County Shopping Center that the REIT still owned in Farmingdale, Long Island, outside its core target area, coincided with it. Management was worried about the undersized, underperforming grocer anchoring that center. UBP sold the seventy-thousand-square-foot shopping center to a local investment group for $9.75 million, representing a profit of about $5.7 million.

With the acquisition of the Dock, the company's cautious approach to adding property in this tough environment for acquisitions had paid off with a 269,000-square-foot facility located on twenty-nine acres, with parking for more than 1,700 cars, making it the fourth largest of UBP's shopping centers. The Dock's commercial potential was also big. The Dock is located in the state's affluent Fairfield County, where the average household income of people living within one mile was $77,383 in 2004. Built on the Housatonic River, at the junction of I-95 and Route 110 in the desirable Route 1 corridor, it was also unique among shopping centers because it had its own marina, large enough to accommodate two hundred boats. To ensure that not only boat owners would patronize its stores, the Dock had as its neighbors, just across the street—Wal-Mart, Home Depot, and Shaw's Supermarket.

UBP's careful research into potential acquisitions and its aggressive approach to converting that potential into reality were responsible for this acquisition. The previous owners, a family that had controlled the location for several generations, had not been in the market to sell and considered the transaction only when UBP approached them.

The Dock had been built in 1971 on the site of an old coal yard and expanded in 1986. With a current roster of fourteen tenants, but also with a large vacant space formerly occupied by a Bradlees Department Store, the Dock was actually two centers, with the smaller anchored by a Super Stop & Shop, which accounted for sixty thousand square feet. Blockbuster Video was another large tenant in that section, which also contained a number of basic service stores, including a cleaners and a pizzeria. Staples and a Petco store anchored the larger section, which also included a Jo-Ann Fabrics store. Petco was truly a national chain, with about 850 stores located in virtually every state. Founded forty years before, the company was known for its commitment to animal rights. It was headquartered in San Diego, where its name was emblazoned on the ballpark used by the San Diego Padres baseball team.

Demonstrating that its acquisition team could also "think small" when appropriate, Urstadt Biddle in 2004 also purchased a group of stores in Rye, New York, one of Westchester's most affluent areas, near the town's main shopping district, adding forty-two thousand square feet of leasable space to its portfolio for just under $11 million. Three of the locations were traditional "street retail" properties, and the fourth was a larger unit known as the Biltmore Shopping Center. UBP already had plans to improve these new additions to its portfolio. Announcing the purchase, UBP president Willing Biddle commented that "well-located street retail can be a fantastic investment," adding that the properties represented "significant upside due to our experienced management and leasing skills." Despite the dearth of parking on local streets compared with that available in shopping centers, the properties represented solid value.

What of the properties already in UBP's portfolio when 2004 began? For most of them, the No Vacancy sign was out. Just short of 99 percent leased, Urstadt Biddle's shopping centers were humming with activity, thanks in large part to the efforts of its leasing division, consisting of UBP vice presidents Linda Lacey and Jim Aries and assistant vice president Charles Davis. What's more, rents on renewed leases were up by a healthy 11 percent over the previous leases. Rents on previously vacant space did even better. In the offing at two of the company's centers was an ideal situation: the Stop & Shop Supermarket in Ossining, New York, and the Shaw's in Darien, Connecticut, each anchoring a center, were in the process of enlarging their locations at their own expense. On the downside, the Southfield, Michigan, office building was still only partly occupied, with a hundred thousand square feet vacant. But to put that troublesome figure in context, the vacancy rate for the office market in the area was an appalling 25 percent, severely limiting leasing possibilities at the time.

In It for the Long Run

Long-distance runners are trained to pause slightly to catch their breath and pace themselves; only sprinters can go all out all the time. Urstadt Biddle Properties was in it for the long run. In 2005 its growth, compared with the pace it had set in the previous few years, slowed. The pause was only evident when comparing 2005 to the company's stellar performance in the preceding years. Under almost any circumstances, 2005 would have been a more-than-satisfactory year, since dividends per share and revenues were up over 2004, while funds from operations dipped only slightly. The latter was a consequence of company compliance with the rigid requirements of the Sarbanes-Oxley law, which cost UBP an additional $700,000 for the year, not to mention the value of the time UBP employees had to spend complying with the new legislation's various provisions.

In fact, UBP's performance over the past few years had begun to attract increasingly favorable attention in the investment community, witness the positive evaluation it received on December 16, 2005, from the popular Web site, the Motley Fool. This Internet-investment-advice Web site wrote that UBP was "certainly worth consideration because of its track record alone." Just as important at a time when investors were paying increased attention to how much accurate and accessible information was available for a company, the Motley Fool also commented: "And for those just starting out following REITs, the company's annual report is very well written and easy to follow." The company itself more than agreed with the Motley Fool's assessment of its prospects, and in October UBP announced a share repurchase program involving up to five hundred thousand shares.

Even one of the "negative" figures posted in 2005—one less office building—was actually a positive development. In June, Urstadt Biddle was finally able to dispose of its prime problem property: the Giffels Building in Southfield, Michigan. For this property, UBP accepted a bit less than it had hoped for, but seen in context, the company did very well. As Willing Biddle explained at a special meeting of the board of directors on May 18, 2005, "the office market remained soft, the property was 50% vacant," and the last tenant in the building "had announced its intention to surrender up to two-thirds of the leased space upon lease expiration in 2007." Compared with UBP's other holdings, a gloomier outlook for a piece of property would be hard to find. Nevertheless, the selling price of $9.75 million represented a company profit of $1.4 million. The sale also meant a reduction in UBP's noncore properties to two distribution centers and one retail property, bringing UBP closer to its goal of being totally concentrated in the Westchester-Putnam-Fairfield counties area.

Also in keeping with company policy of trying to minimize its involvement in partnerships, UBP repurchased, for $2.1 million, outstanding interests in its partnership in the Arcadian Shopping Center in Ossining, thus giving Urstadt Biddle, which had been the general partner, total control of the location. That left UBP with only two general partnerships: the Ridgeway Shopping Center in Stamford and the Shoppes at Eastchester.

Expansion was always on the agenda, even in a slower year. To help fund future purchases, UBP, in April, sold $62 million of Series D senior cumulative preferred stock. "We have money to spend," was UBP president Biddle's summation of the results of the sale.

And spend it it did. UBP added a second large shopping center acquisition in June 2005 for $28.4 million. At two hundred thousand square feet, the Staples Plaza in Yorktown in upper Westchester County, purchased from a private investment group, became UBP's fifth largest location. According to Biddle, "The purchase of Staples Plaza continues our strategic goal to be the dominant retail real estate owner in Westchester County, New York and Fairfield County, Connecticut and adds to the $50 million of retail property purchased earlier this year."

The company's purchase did not include the center's "shadow" anchor, a BJ's Wholesale Club; but among the tenants in the part of the property it now owned were the ubiquitous Staples, Bed Bath & Beyond, Party City, Dunkin Donuts, and AC Moore. The last was a chain of crafts stores that had begun in Moorestown, New Jersey, in 1985. A featured product at the store was scrapbooking supplies, plugging into a hobby that was becoming very popular.

The 16.4-acre Staples Plaza, 97 percent leased at the time of purchase, with basement warehouse space leased to Best Plumbing Tile & Stone, had begun in the 1960s with a White's Department Store and Waldbaum's supermarket and expanded in later decades with the emphasis on home improvement stores. While not on the busier Route 6 corridor, its location on Route 202, less than a mile from the Taconic Parkway, could be a positive since, as Biddle remarked at the time, the Route 6 corridor "can become such a congested traffic nightmare that it's a turnoff to a lot of people." Further, Yorktown's recent moratorium on new development was set to expire soon after UBP's purchase, thus suggesting an upside for future development at the center.

Meanwhile, significant activity continued at other properties UBP already owned. For example, at the recently purchased Westchester Pavilion in White Plains, the departure of an OfficeMax was the occasion to welcome a new tenant to replace it: Daffy's, a discount designer clothing and home goods store very much in tune with the times. In existence forty-four years and now counting twenty stores with annual revenues upward of $160 million, Daffy's, the first clothing store to locate at the pavilion, was a retailer that posed the threat of temptation to consumers at every turn. The *New York Times*, writing about this new Daffy's outlet, quoted a nearby office worker: "It's going to be dangerously close to where I work. Maybe I'd better lock up my credit cards." Daffy's thus fit perfectly into UBP's desired mix of retailers looking for value-oriented stores, where one could grab a clothing bargain and then lunch on a Subway sandwich.

Also typical of how UBP upgraded its purchases was the current renovation of the Pavilion. Sometimes just adding carpeting in the right spots can give a mall a different "feel," and the company was doing just that in the Pavilion's public areas. It was also providing more seats while increasing amenities such as food kiosks, where a sushi outlet would add an international flavor, tapping into current tastes. The company was also considering the advantage of the synergy that could come from possibly adding a child care center, thus drawing more women customers who would shop in stores such as Daffy's. As Willing Biddle summed up UBP's reasoning: "Our stores had been hard-goods. We wanted to get a soft-goods retailer to have a broader tenant base and attract different types of shoppers. We concluded that if we can get more women to come into the shopping center, it would benefit all of our stores there."

Throughout UBP's shopping centers in 2005, rents on renewals were up 6 percent, while vacant space was rented for about 10 percent more than it had previously been bringing in. If the percentage of space leased company-wide fell by a percent, from 99 to 98 percent, the context, on the edge of perfection, made the drop easier to bear. Also encouraging was the fact that at the Goodwives Shopping Center in Darien—the new, renovated Shaw's Supermarket—reopened for business in the facility that the retailer had paid for itself.

A pleasant sidelight of 2005 was the awarding in October of the Steven L. Newman Real Estate Institute's first annual Award for Visionary Leadership in Real Estate to company chairman and CEO Charles J. Urstadt for his leadership as first chairman and chief executive officer of the Battery Park City Authority in New York City in the 1970s. Almost single-handedly responsible for starting, obtaining funding and filling in the hundred acres in the Hudson River off lower Manhattan, Urstadt had continued to serve on that board, although in recent years in a reduced capacity as vice chairman so as to devote full time to Urstadt Biddle Properties.

The success and expansion of UBP in the half-decade after the millennium was built on such solid foundations that when, inevitably, its rate of growth slowed for a spell, it showed up merely as a pause, not a decline. The year 2006 continued the slower growth pattern established in 2005, but the two years together looked ordinary only compared with the rapid growth pace in the preceding years. Most companies, after all, would have regarded it as a pretty good year when they could lead off an annual report with the statement: "2006 was earmarked by a stable leasing record and modest growth for the Company." Urstadt Biddle could have kept buying shopping centers at the rate to which its shareholders had become accustomed, but the high prices such properties were carrying were out of sync with the earnings returns the company could reasonably anticipate from them. At the board of directors meeting on September 7, 2006, CEO Urstadt reported that besides higher prices "the Company was seeing lower same property net operating income and lower returns on recent acquisitions."

If things were, of necessity, relatively quiet on the acquisitions front, the direction for UBP was still forward. In March, Urstadt Biddle announced the purchase of three properties, spending $16.6 million when it closed on them three months later. The acquisitions added 47,300 square feet of leasable space to the company portfolio.

The centerpiece of these purchases from a private investor was the twenty-five-thousand-square-foot Gristede's Shopping Center on the Boston Post Road (US 1) in Pelham Manor in Westchester County. Located in one of the more affluent suburbs immediately adjacent to New York City, the center, anchored by a Gristede's supermarket and including a Dunkin' Donuts and a Bank of America branch among its tenants, needed some cosmetic work on its facade to bring it up to par and make it capable of producing higher rents in the future.

The other properties involved in the transaction, which UBP had to buy as part of the package, consisted of two twelve-thousand-square-foot groups of fully leased blockfront retail stores housing about twenty local retailers in the stable working class neighborhood of the Flushing section of Queens in New York City. Flushing presented a densely populated, desirable New York City neighborhood that never seemed to have enough retail outlets to fill the areas' increasing shopping needs.

The rising cost of prime properties naturally increased the value of the assets already in UBP's portfolio, at least on paper. More important in terms of cash flow and, ultimately, annual FFO was the company's leasing picture. On this front, big-box store bankruptcies still presented problems, largely accounting for a slight slip, from the previous year's 98 percent to 2006's 97 percent of space leased. On the positive side, the LA Fitness facility at the Ridgeway Shopping Center finally opened. In addition, several major leases turned over at significantly higher rents. Major renovation work completed or cleared to begin at the Arcadian and the Dock shopping centers offered the promise of greater revenues from these properties in the very near future. Parts of the UBP properties in Springfield and Meriden, with the addition of new construction, were already producing higher revenue or would be doing so by the end of 2007.

With Sarbanes-Oxley presenting an ongoing drain on the resources of all small-cap companies, economizing, without hurting the bottom line, was a must. In January 2006, as part of its cost-cutting programs that would be stepped up throughout the year, Urstadt Biddle Properties changed auditors, ending its relationship with Ernst & Young and beginning one with PKF, Certified Public Accountants. Besides reducing the fixed expense of auditing, the new relationship also promised to provide better response time from the auditor.

This "average" year of 2006 at Urstadt Biddle produced a few cents less per share in net income, but higher prices for both the company's and Class A common stock. Total revenue was up, although FFO dipped a bit, the consequence not of lower rents but the continuing pressure of bankruptcy-created vacancies. While it had surely become a cliché at UBP, it was a cliché that no one tired of repeating: dividends increased for the thirteen consecutive year. After thirty-seven years of operation, UBP had never skipped a dividend, nor was there any prospect of that happening in the foreseeable future.

The company's performance during 2007 was excellent, with every important statistic trending upward. FFO per share increased by almost 8 percent; total revenues were up to a new high of $75.9 million, representing an increase of nearly 5 percent over 2006; and UBP secured an average increase of 11 percent on new leases and 13 percent on renewals. One statistic that didn't increase was overhead expenses. For the year, UBP paid a dividend per share of $0.92 on Class A common stock and $0.83 on the company's common stock. It marked the fourteenth consecutive year of dividend increases.

In a difficult acquisition environment, the company was nevertheless able to profitably add to its holdings with two strategic purchases that fit in perfectly with its core business plan. UBP's purchase of the ninety-two-thousand-square-foot Emerson Plaza in Emerson, New Jersey, added a shopping center in the upper income New York City suburb of Bergen County. Built in the 1980s, the center is anchored by a fifty-thousand-square-foot ShopRite Supermarket and also houses Dunkin' Donuts, Hallmark Cards, Bank of America, and H&R Block locations.

Joining Emerson in the Urstadt Biddle portfolio was Starbucks Plaza, a convenience shopping center in Monroe, Connecticut, in Fairfield County, anchored by a Starbucks store. A modest, newly built facility, the center occupied about two acres and contained just over ten thousand square feet of leasable space. Willing Biddle characterized it as "very functional and well located on a busy commuter thoroughfare and the tenants provide a good mix of basic services." At the Shoppes at Eastchester in New York's Westchester County, UBP bought out the limited partner interest it did not already own and also acquired a 20 percent interest in a retail office property in affluent Bronxville in Westchester County.

At the Dock—in Stamford, Connecticut, where 107,000 square feet had been left vacant by the failure of Bradlees—UBP replaced the departed tenant with a BJ's Wholesale Club. Another departure was also a profitable move for Urstadt Biddle, which sold its 126,000-square-foot Tempe, Arizona, property for a gain of $11.4 million.

A Foundation for the Future

Two important themes have characterized the operation of Urstadt Biddle Properties since it began to take on its modern form and direction in the late 1980s. One is steady growth, always with an eye to the company's general strategy of focusing its efforts on a core of supermarket-anchored shopping centers in the affluent areas of Westchester, Putnam, and Fairfield counties in New York and Connecticut. The other is a willingness to be flexible enough, within that strategy, to take advantage of attractive opportunities and also to adapt to whatever change and challenges technology, demography, and the general business climate present.

Company president Willing Biddle summed up the UBP experience in a 2006 newspaper interview: "You don't have to be huge to be successful." As 2008 began, Urstadt Biddle Properties, with thirty-two employees working out of part of a two-story company-owned office building in Greenwich, in which it occupied about 5,000 square feet, owned or had interests in a portfolio of thirty-two retail properties and six office buildings totaling close to 4 million square feet with a book value of about $471 million. Close to 90 percent of the UBP portfolio was located in a core area where the median annual income was just above $70,000, compared with $45,500 for the rest of the nation. Restrictive zoning in UBP's three main target counties has held square footage devoted to retail stores to not much more than half the average per county found in other parts of the country, pricing shopping space at a premium.

Perhaps nothing reflected as much on the company's solidity as what UBP was proud to announce at the beginning of 2008. With the subprime crisis building to a peak and credit tightening to the point where even some major credit-worthy businesses were having trouble securing financing, UBP had achieved the ultimate vote of confidence: a $50 million unsecured revolving credit agreement with the Bank of New York Mellon and Wells Fargo Bank, N.A., guaranteeing the company access to funds at favorable terms and rates whenever promising acquisition possibilities presented themselves. A month later, UBP sold $60 million of cumulative preferred stock in a private placement to WFC Holdings Corporation, a holding company for Wells Fargo Bank, N.A.

Although the company's time-tested business strategy certainly provided a template for the future, management continued to fine-tune and adapt it to changing times. A difficult acquisitions environment suggested that a greater use of partnerships might prove more fruitful, and UBP became more open to such arrangements. UBP was also making a foray into opportunities that it had previously considered but never extensively exploited, including leveraging its managerial expertise to bring in revenue from the management of property owned by other companies.

With a proven business plan, a solid history of dividends combined with mostly steady growth and a management team with many years of experience that had taken nary a misstep, the company had finally established itself with Wall Street. Its preferred stock retained its BB rating, and the price of its common shares remained healthy. The next generation of management was not only in place but had already proven its mettle. CEO Charles J. Urstadt, who in 2005 had been honored with the first Award for Visionary Leadership in Real Estate by the Steven L. Newman Real Estate Institute at Baruch College in New York City, summed it up when he described UBP President Wing Biddle as "the finest real estate man" he had ever known.

There was thus every reason to believe that the future would bring a continuation of past achievements. And given the company's history, that was bound to be a very good thing.

Chapter Seven

SUCCESSFULLY NEGOTIATING TOUGH TIMES

With more cash-strapped consumers going back to shopping for basics, the neighborhood shopping center is gaining ground over chi-chi lifestyle centers and suburban malls.

This gives real-estate investment trusts investing in grocery store-anchored strip malls . . . a competitive edge in the broader retail REIT universe, rattled by rising vacancy rates and retailer bankruptcies.

The Wall Street Journal, October 15, 2008

Urstadt Biddle Properties' business plan, which had proved successful throughout many ordinary business cycles over several decades, was eminently qualified to cope with the extraordinary economic circumstances alluded to in the quotation above from *The Wall Street Journal*. Moreover, the path laid out by the company's CEO, Charles J. Urstadt—concentrating on core properties consisting of neighborhood shopping centers in the affluent fifty mile radius from its Greenwich, Connecticut headquarters, minimizing it's participation in partnerships that it did not control, limiting debt financing (72 percent of the forty-four properties owned in 2008 were free of mortgages) and pursuing new opportunities only when they promised to add real value and enhance Urstadt Biddle's ability to keep paying dividends—indeed, to increase dividends—made the company fitter than most to ride out any stretch of rough weather. As it happens, it was tailor-made to survive the perfect storm that was looming in 2008, even though the new commercial landscape partly created by the extended economic downturn would eventually make it necessary for the company to fine tune its business plan.

In fact, UBP's performance in "The Great Recession" that was soon to engulf the country was the answer to those who had questioned that business plan. In the go-go boom years of the early 2000s, some had criticized Urstadt Biddle's conservative approach to growth. With banks aggressively pushing loans, especially for real estate, "slow and steady" seemed simply old-fashioned. Perhaps it was, but in those years, so was common sense. "Liars" mortgages were putting families in homes they clearly could not afford (but only minimally in the area where UBP's portfolio of shopping centers was located) and developers of commercial real estate competed to fill every inch of space in questionable markets with new office buildings, hotels and shopping centers, many of them heavily leveraged. The loans that supported this building frenzy were themselves heavily leveraged, securitized and re-securitized to such an extent that it was often hard to figure out what had happened to the original loan. But it wasn't hard to get a read on this business environment and the mentality of many consumers and business people: anything goes and never mind that rainy day because it's always fair weather.

That Rainy Day Becomes The Perfect Storm

To evaluate the performance of any business, one has to look at many factors, including its business plan, the ability and knowledge of its management and employees, the company's capitalization and access to new capital, its assets, the changing nature of its industry and market, new technology and changing tastes, the competition and the relevant demographic factors related to its customer base. But all of this plays out within a business environment over which no management has control. And in the period 2008-2009, everything for awhile seemed to be out of control.

The residential sub-prime mortgage crisis that had been building to a crescendo in 2007 produced havoc in 2008, threatening shopping center REITs as much as any other type of business. Residential foreclosures became a news staple, not only hurting people directly affected but also, combined with a deteriorating employment picture, frightening homeowners in arrears and worrying just about everyone who had to make a monthly mortgage payment. Worried people buy less. Lower sales forced some retail companies into bankruptcy, which then closed stores. Shopping center owners, faced with increasing vacancies, were hard pressed to negotiate higher rents and indeed often had to grant concessions to keep good tenants. Banks became unwilling to grant credit to all but their very best customers and the credit market froze up—very bad news for REITs that depended on leverage to grow and pay dividends. Some large, highly leveraged shopping center owners had to sell off assets to finance current needs. The price of gas spiked. While that favored some neighborhood shopping centers because people sought to conserve fuel, it also made consumers feel less wealthy, causing them to cut back on spending. Also affecting consumer outlook was a stock market that by the end of the year seemed to be in freefall, prompting nervous jokes about 401-k plans becoming "201-k plans."

Urstadt Biddle's *2008 Annual Report* put it succinctly: "The U. S. economy is facing challenges not previously experienced during our lifetimes." The particulars were sobering, and by the fall of 2008 would become out and out scary. Although it would be almost 2009 before we knew that the recession had officially begun at the beginning of 2008, everyone knew it had arrived long before it was a matter of record. The Fed, spotting big trouble, lowered interest rates twice in nine days in January 2008. Monthly retail sales figures in February dropped "the most in five years," a phrase that would become commonplace every month for a few months until it got even worse later in the year. Before February was over, General Motors would announce the biggest annual loss ever for any automobile manufacturer.

March saw Bear Stearns on the edge of a precipice and then sold to J. P. Morgan Chase for a pittance through a government arranged merger, shaking Wall Street. Despite being as well situated as any other REIT to cope with the crisis, Urstadt Biddle was beginning to feel the heat. At its Board meeting on March 6, company president Willing Biddle reported that Staples and Panera Bread had withdrawn plans to expand in the company's centers until the economic outlook "improved." He also reported that Hollywood Video, with stores in two centers was sliding into bankruptcy and that Border's was closing its store in the big Urstadt Biddle center in White Plains, New York. The company's occupancy rate was still at 95.5 percent, but that would be the peak for some time to come.

By May the Fed had dropped interest rates seven times in the previous eight months, but consumers still weren't borrowing and banks weren't lending. Among the bankruptcies announced that month was that of Linen 'N Things, an Urstadt Biddle tenant at two locations. "The climate has really shifted since last November, which is when retailers saw their world start to collapse," *National Real Estate Investor* quoted one analyst on the tenor of the times. Also in May, when good weather traditionally has Americans increasing their time behind the wheel, driving declined for the first time for that month since 1979, a bad omen for many shopping centers.

In June, again for the first time, drivers paid $4 a gallon at the pump while the jobless rate leaped half a point to 5.5 percent, the largest spike in any month since 1988. On June 5, the Urstadt Biddle Board of Directors officially was informed that Safavieh, the rug and furniture chain, had closed its store in a company shopping center and Chairman Urstadt noted that it was becoming harder to conclude leases on favorable terms.

By July even Starbucks was closing stores around the country. Foreclosures continued to increase and "under water" became a common term on the nightly news to describe many homeowners, whose mortgage balances were now higher than the value of their homes. The next month the federal government seized Fannie Mae and Freddie Mac.

In September, in one horrific weekend, Lehman Brothers was reported to be on the verge of liquidation and the iconic Merrill Lynch, which four decades previously had launched the predecessor of Urstadt Biddle Properties, Hubbard Real Estate Investments, was taken over by Bank of America. A few days later the government had to bail out AIG, the insurance behemoth. Bailouts would follow for the auto industry—and a week later, under government supervision, Goldman Sachs and Morgan Stanley became bank-holding companies, no longer independent brokerages. Almost as a footnote as the month ended, Washington Mutual became the largest bank failure in American history.

The Urstadt Biddle Board meeting in September was held in the shadow of national uncertainty and fear. The bad news this time was that company tenant KB Toys had closed two stores. With characteristic calmness, Chairman Urstadt reassured the Board that there was no cause for alarm as the company maintained a strong balance sheet and continued to devote special attention to those centers where vacancies exist.

But for many Americans, the worst was yet to come. For consumers, without whom shopping centers would have no reason to exist, October was possibly the most frightening month. There were two indices that gave Americans a good sense of their wealth. One was the value of their home, for some time on a downward slope. In addition, through their 401-k plans, union, state and municipal pension funds, mutual funds and ownership of individual stocks, Americans had come to gauge the health of the economy and their personal prospects by one number: the Dow Jones industrials average. It had opened the year at over 13,000. But in a series of sickeningly steep plunges, especially late in the trading session on many days in mid-October, the Dow Jones, which had been ratcheting down most of the year, at one point dropped below 8,500, and some analysts were predicting a 6,000 Dow.

To top it off, as consumer prices tallied their biggest one-month drop since World War II, the word "deflation," so redolent of the bitter Depression of the 1930s, was in the air. Certainly the half a million people who lost their jobs in December could believe that the threads that tied production, investment and consumption together might be unraveling.

It hardly even seems appropriate to call this a "business environment" at all. Urstadt Biddle Properties' senior management had for many years made the point that its steady approach to growth, light leverage and emphasis on the basics was not only the most sensible way to run a real estate investment trust over time, it was also the most prudent way to do well in the inevitable bad times as well as the good. These were the worst of times, so to paraphrase former New York City mayor Edward Koch, now that the acid test had presented itself, how was the company doing?

Under the circumstances, UBP was performing quite well, if not without a few hitches, and very well compared to all other REITs, especially similar firms that owned neighborhood shopping centers. At the company's Board meeting on December 10, Charles Urstadt was able to report "that among retail REITs the company was the only one with a positive return to investors." He acknowledged that, given the trajectory of the economy, tenants would fail. He also noted that senior management was especially vigilant at this time about holding down administrative expenses. But overall, since Urstadt Biddle did not depend on just a few large retailers for its revenue stream and had conservatively managed its growth with a relatively light debt load, it was not only riding out the storm but even in an excellent position to take advantage of any opportunities to acquire properties that seemed likely to come on the market at favorable prices, given the severe downturn.

While it may not have been evident during 2008, which seemed at the time like a perpetual hurricane of bad news, UBP actually had a year that was not too far out of the ordinary, and that was good news. The company continued to grow and it continued its uninterrupted flow of dividends. If some of the numbers in its annual report were a little on the flat side, that wasn't such a bad thing when everyone else's numbers seemed to go nowhere but down. As President Willing Biddle remarked, for the time, "flat was the new 'good'."

For several years Urstadt Biddle had slowed acquisitions, unwilling to overpay for properties that did not represent real value. And the company began 2008 modestly, closing on a 20,000 square foot property in Waldwick, in Bergen County, New Jersey, the prosperous suburb just across the Hudson from New York City, where a stable and affluent population was increasingly making it a target for UBP acquisitions. The price was $6.25 million for the site, occupied by a Rite-Aid drugstore. This was a forward-looking move encompassing plans to ultimately redevelop and add retail space. Meanwhile this Rite-Aid, with a net lease that ran through 2017, would propitiously enhance company cash flow.

In February, with times already looking very bad, UBP drew upon one of its most important assets: its reputation. The credit market was already going into its deep freeze, but not for *this* REIT. Urstadt Biddle Properties concluded a $50 million unsecured revolving credit agreement (which under certain circumstances could reach $100 million) at a historically low interest rate with The Bank of New York Mellon and Wells Fargo Bank N. A. "In the currently challenging credit environment it is important that we have immediate access to funds at favorable terms and rates in order to help us capitalize on what we believe will be an improving real estate acquisitions market in the near term," commented Willing Biddle. Three months later Urstadt Biddle was able to extend into 2011 a separate $30 million secured revolving credit facility it had previously obtained from The Bank of New York Mellon.

By all rights the acquisitions market should have improved, but if that was going to happen, the signs of more favorable prices were not yet there. In fact, what should have been a consequence of the prolonged downturn in the economy, lower prices for even prime locations, would prove to be very stubborn in making an appearance. With population static in its traditional region for acquisitions, the company now turned to an area of northern New Jersey that offered considerable promise: the Ironbound section of Newark. This part of the city had long avoided the problems of some of the city's other neighborhoods, being literally self-contained and separated from the outside by boundaries of surrounding railroads. Originally settled by people of Portuguese descent, the population was now a solid mix of blue collar and increasingly upper middle class consumers.

The shopping center was Ferry Plaza, a property that had come to the attention of UBP through its close relationship with Howard Menaker, a part owner of the property and a former limited partner in the limited partnership through which the company, six years earlier, had acquired it's largest asset—the Ridgeway Shopping Center in Stamford, CT. Just over 100,000 square feet and anchored by a Pathmark supermarket, part of the A&P chain, which accounted for about 63,000 square feet of that total footage, Ferry Plaza was 95 percent leased and also included Subway, Carvel, GNC, Blockbuster Video, Dots, Rainbow and a branch of the Valley National Bank. With an existing mortgage of $11.9 million, the center was valued at $26 million. Urstadt Biddle used a subsidiary to acquire a 60 percent interest through a limited partnership, making use of $8.7 million from its recent sale of preferred stock.

In August the company acquired from a family-owned investment fund the 79,000-square foot Veterans Plaza Shopping Center, located in New Milford, Connecticut. The center was anchored by a Big Y supermarket, one of a chain of stores in Connecticut and Massachusetts, with locations concentrated in the Connecticut River Valley. Founded in 1936, the business was named for the location of the first supermarket it owned in Chicopee, Massachusetts, at the convergence of two roads. The $10.3 million UBP paid for the shopping center was financed by the company's March sale of preferred stock and also involved the assumption of a $3.6 million first mortgage. Most importantly, given the tenor of the times, the property was 100 percent leased. Other tenants included a Rite-Aid pharmacy and a Danbury Savings Bank branch.

Looking toward future expansion, the company also bought two former Chase Manhattan bank branches in Westchester County. The package purchase was made with the particular goal of securing one of the properties, which was adjacent to Urstadt Biddle's Chilmark Shopping Center. The company then moved to sell off the other property.

In a year in which negative numbers seemed to rule the business world, Urstadt Biddle produced a balance sheet that was remarkably "balanced." True, FFO was down 1 percent per share, but that was partly caused by the redemption of preferred stock. Between its revolving credit agreement and the March sale of $60 million of preferred stock, Urstadt Biddle had a potential war chest of more than $100 million dollars. If there would be bargains out there, this company could and would be a buyer. But there would also be competition, partly from REITs that were willing to leverage with abandon. In May, *National Real Estate Investor* noted that some REITs were refinancing assets, "using their portfolios like ATM machines to strengthen balance sheets and fund growth." That was the very practice that had gotten many homeowners in trouble in recent years.

Urstadt Biddle rental revenues were up 6.5 percent in 2008, although tenant bankruptcies—which included Hancock Fabrics in addition to those previously mentioned—suggested that this figure could take a hit in the next year or two. And in the midst of something of a leasing panic among many retail REITs, the company nevertheless was able to fill its largest vacancy, a 100,000 square foot space that was vacated by a bankrupt former tenant at the Dock Shopping Center in Stratford, Connecticut. Although UBP had been receiving rent on the vacant space through a guaranty of the former tenant's obligations, it used the proceeds from a lease termination agreement to raze the vacant space and provide BJ's Warehouse Club with a significant allowance to construct a new 107,000 square foot warehouse club that became a major anchor for the center. Most satisfyingly, UBP was able to increase annual dividends for both Common and Class A Common stock—this at a time when one out of every four REITs had decreased dividends.

In contrast with these results produced by a policy of slow, prudent and steady growth, investors were reading in the financial press as the year ended that General Growth Properties, the name of which aptly reflected the first priority of the highly leveraged, second biggest mall owner in America, had not only dropped its dividend but was also having to sell its properties in Las Vegas to raise $1.75 billion to cover loans coming due in 2008. In fact, they were on their way to bankruptcy.

The middle of a financial crisis is a difficult time to change chief financial officers, which is why Urstadt Biddle was fortunate that when James Moore, who had held that position since 1989, retired in June, he was replaced by John Hayes, a CPA who had joined the company the previous year. Hayes had been with the accounting firm of PKF and had also served as corporate controller for a private commercial real estate company and a company that owned and operated large format laundromats. Chairman Charles J. Urstadt said of Hayes that he had "demonstrated outstanding ability to carry out the duties of our CFO." And with the addition to the Urstadt Biddle Board of Directors in 2008 of Kevin J. Bannon, former chief investment officer of The Bank of New York, the company further bolstered its fund of knowledge and experience in preparation for the still rough times to come. And come they would, for while 2009 would not bring as many dramatic daily headlines as 2008, it would manifest the wreckage one might expect in the wake of a storm. With the Dow Jones Equity REIT Index down 40 percent for the year, what would be next? On New Year's Eve, *The Wall Street Journal* warned that "real-estate investment trusts are bracing for a Darwinian 2009."

The Morning After

"Property transactions have come to nearly a complete halt," *Barron's* quoted an analyst on February 2, 2009. "The market has discounted REIT shares to levels that anticipate a drawn-out period of deteriorating fundamentals. They are trading at steep discounts to asset values, even using our reduced estimates of value, historically high dividend yields and low price to cash flow multiples. The single most important factor affecting a recovery will be the course of the economy."

Many REITs were struggling. KIMCO, which years ago had failed in a hostile bid to take over Urstadt Biddle, was now besieged by $7.5 billion in debt and was looking at an 81 percent drop in the value of its stock over the past year. Columbus, Ohio-based Glimcher Realty Trust had recently sold six of its shopping malls to keep afloat. Even the stock of Federal Realty, a pillar of strength compared to some other REITs, was selling at only about 75 percent of net asset value reported *National Real Estate Investor* in May.

At the Urstadt Biddle Board of Directors' meeting on March 5, 2009, company president Willing Biddle acknowledged "a very challenging retail market." The economy, still struggling to get moving again, was kinder to Urstadt Biddle than to many other REITs because of the company's mix of tenants. Supermarkets, casual dining and sporting goods were holding their own, while discretionary purchases such as jewelry were off. Among many of Urstadt Biddle's tenants—forty-five in the first quarter—rent adjustments had become a high priority. While trying to hold the line on rent reductions, Biddle reported, the company was willing to negotiate on deferrals in return for tenant concessions.

Acquisitions remained problematic, despite the company's solid cash position. James Aries, Senior Vice President of Acquisitions and Leasing, told the Board that he was seeing "a disconnect between the value we assign to properties and their asking price, sometimes representing a spread of as much as 200 basis points over capitalization rates." This was something of a surprise, given all the suggestions in the business press that this would be a good time for REITs to go bargain hunting.

Members of the Urstadt Biddle Board of Directors were themselves holding the line. They voted not to emulate some other REITs that were paying dividends in the form of stock rather than cash. The company's now forty-year tradition of uninterrupted cash dividends would continue.

UBP's *2009 Annual Report* appropriately began with the famous line from Dickens' *Tale of Two Cities*, "It was the best of times, it was the worst of times. . . ." Although not its first concern, the value of Urstadt Biddle stock had held up well compared to the competition and, most importantly, the dividend checks kept coming. Indeed, at the Board meeting on June 4, Chairman Charles Urstadt reported that Deutsche Bank Securities had emphasized the company's favorable return compared to similar REITs and he observed that unlike UBP, other companies were either having trouble initiating a stock offering or had to accept low share prices. But it was also a time, as the annual report noted, when "retailers have been more focused on survival than expansion." Inevitably that was reflected in Urstadt Biddle's occupancy rate, which at one point in the year dipped close to 90 percent before finishing 2009 at just over 92 percent.

By mid-2009, investors were so relieved that REITs—at least most of them—had not actually faced Armageddon or fallen off the ends of the Earth, that share prices made a considerable recovery. But stock prices, as Charles Urstadt was fond of saying, were a matter of opinion. Actual business at shopping centers was still off, current tenants were still struggling and new leases at favorable rents were going to be a tough sell for the foreseeable future.

As 2009 progressed, more REITs were able to sell stock to raise capital for expansion and balance sheet recapitalization, and the property bargains that had been forecast at the depth of the recession seemed to be moving farther and farther away. At the Urstadt Biddle Board of Directors meeting on September 15, UBP's chairman, celebrating twenty years as its CEO, told the members that "the company has weathered the recession well." Still, Mr. Urstadt had to admit that despite the company's $20 million in cash and a current $70 million line of credit, he had a paucity of news to report in terms of new acquisitions or even anything in the pipeline. In fact, 2009 would be the quietest year in that area of the Company's operations since 1995. Urstadt Biddle Properties grew by only three bank branch buildings in 2009, adding not a single shopping center.

Nevertheless UBP was creative in adding and protecting shareholder value in 2009. Late in the year a movie theater in its Shop-Rite Center in Carmel, New York failed. With Christmas approaching, quick action was required since this was a business that helped produce traffic for other retailers at the shopping center. UBP quickly formed a subsidiary to temporarily operate the theater, hired a manager who could get the job done and reopened it in time for the rush of traditional Christmas films that drew families to the theater and the rest of the stores in the shopping center. A policy of hiring some employees with disabilities to work in that theater even garnered a humanitarian award for UBP. (The state of Connecticut also honored the company in 2009 with an environmental award for reducing energy consumption—and costs—at its Ridgeway Shopping Center in Stamford.)

The theater would shortly be sold to a more appropriate owner, but its purchase and brief operation by Urstadt Biddle was indicative of the advantages of the company's business plan, which was to keep tight control of operations by restricting the purchase of property to an area that could be reached in a brief trip from company headquarters and also by running the company with a staff just big enough to get the job done. The upshot was flexibility and the capability to quickly assess a problem and act just as quickly to successfully resolve it.

Nobody had expected 2009 to be a stellar year. Company president and chief operating officer Willing Biddle, surveying the REIT's performance in December in the wake of "The Great Recession," commented:

> Although 2009 was one of the most challenging years the commercial real estate industry has ever faced, we feel that UBP navigated the challenge as well as, if not better than, any other shopping center REIT. Our FFO was relatively flat, while many of our competitors FFO's were down significantly when compared with 2008. Many of our competitors were forced to issue equity to de-leverage their balance sheets at extremely dilutive prices, but we had no need to do so due to our conservative management philosophy over many years. We retained full access to the credit markets as evidenced by the two mortgage financings that we completed in 2009 at industry leading rates. Although we were disappointed that we were unable to continue our growth of the last several years by acquiring additional grocery anchored shopping centers; we are well prepared to do so. UBP has over $10 million in cash on hand and over $80 million available under its two existing lines of credit that do not expire until 2011 and 2013. During 2009 we renewed or signed new leases for 602,000 square feet of space or nearly 15.4% of our gross leasable space. Overall the rental rate on our renewals represented average rent increases of 4.5%. Given the market place we were glad to see our rental rate on new leases decrease by only 8.3%. Overall our percentage of space leased in our core portfolio fell 2.4% during the year to end at 92.1% due primarily to two tenant bankruptcies and store closures resulting from retail restructurings coupled with reduced demand by retailers to open new stores in this very uncertain time.

In 2009, the great majority of publicly traded retail REITs lowered or eliminated their dividends. Many REITs were focusing on conserving capital and the easiest way to do this was to take it from the dividends their shareholders were expecting. In October, *Real Estate Finance* reported that decreased dividends had, on the average, produced about $2 billion dollars per quarter for all REITs. But not for the shopping center REIT in Greenwich, Connecticut, which had generated more than sufficient capital to meet its needs by effectively running its business. In December, in fact, Urstadt Biddle's Board of Directors voted a dividend increase of a penny per share on Common and Class A Common stock.

By 2010 the recession had begun to recede, but much more slowly than most people expected, and its shadow lingered in the form of reduced consumption almost across the board. As an analyst colorfully put it to *The Wall Street Journal* in February, "We're not [returning] to the shopaholic days of yesterday." For years the pundits had complained that Americans weren't saving enough, that they had been too free with their ubiquitous credit and debit cards. Now businesses would have to work that much harder to get their customers to make the purchases they had been making so freely for the past decade.

All the more reason for a company whose business was buying, tenanting, improving and running neighborhood shopping centers to maintain its conservative mode of operation, emphasizing supermarkets and drugstores, which could easily account for 60 to 70 percent of a shopping center's income and which were stores people kept patronizing in bad times and good. Reason as well to maintain the company's geographical orientation. With national unemployment at an average 9.8 percent for 2010, the four counties in which Urstadt Biddle concentrated its business—Bergen, Fairfield, Putnam and Westchester—came in at 7.2 percent.

In that conservative vein, 2010 began prosaically, with the company re-leasing the only non-core properties surviving from that long-ago time when Urstadt Biddle's predecessor, Hubbard Real Estate Investments, was literally all over the map. In February, Chrysler signed a new lease on its UBP-owned warehouse facilities in the Dallas and St. Louis areas. Rents from these non-core properties were slightly down, but given the shaky period the U. S. auto industry had just survived (barely), the deal was a satisfactory one. Meanwhile, the company's intent would continue to be to sell the properties, but only when a reasonable offer presented itself.

UBP's leasing group, headed by senior vice president Linda Lacey, had their work cut out for them, since the space vacated in 2009 by Linen N'Things, Border's, and Fortunoff' accounted for nearly 100,000 square feet. By March, overall leased space was up, and at 93.6 percent was not far from the 95 percent level that Urstadt Biddle had typically maintained in better times. Just as importantly, overall rent revenue on both lease renewals and newly rented vacant space rose.

In April, 2010, Urstadt Biddle began to grow again, ending a year-long virtual moratorium on property purchases. The first of several major acquisitions it would make that year was the Putnam Plaza Shopping Center in Carmel, New York, which President Willing Biddle characterized as "the most dominant grocery anchored shopping center in Carmel." Again, the company resourced long-established business acquaintances, this time with Mr. Josh Goldberg who owned the property, to create a co-tenancy through which a wholly owned subsidiary of the company would become the owner of a two-thirds interest in yet another supermarket-anchored shopping center. The Hannaford Brothers Supermarket, part of the Delaize Group, anchored the 20-acre center that contributed another 193,000 square feet of rentable space to UBP's inventory. New York Sports Health Club was another major tenant. Other stores included Dress Barn, Radio Shack, Rite-Aid, and Starbucks.

UBP almost simultaneously made a smaller, less costly purchase, but one that was located in an area of similarly upscale population. The company again used a wholly owned subsidiary to acquire 28,000 square feet of mixed use property only two blocks from the Metro North railroad station in Katonah, New York and Route 684, the most important highway in the area. A quarter of the rentals here would come from office space, the rest from retail, which featured a Mrs. Green's Natural Food Market. Mr. Biddle noted of the new company property that Katonah was in the town of Bedford, "which has one of the nation's highest average household incomes." Together, the April acquisitions in Carmel and Katonah were 95 percent leased, a good figure in the wake of the severe economic setback the country had just passed through.

Hardly had these deals been finalized when Urstadt Biddle was again a buyer. In May it was along Route 7 north of Danbury, Connecticut in New Milford. The New Milford Plaza, anchored by a Super Stop & Shop and a Wal-Mart, offered 231,000 square feet of leasable space on its twenty-two acres. Other tenants included GameShop, Radio Shack, Hallmark, Dollar Tree and a branch of the Union Savings Bank. With the purchase, Urstadt Biddle now owned most of the supermarket-anchored space in the area.

Completing one of the most productive three-month periods for acquisitions in the company's history, Urstadt Biddle in June added to its roster a twenty-five percent partnership interest in the Midway Shopping Center in affluent Scarsdale, New York. Located on twenty-nine prime acres on Central Park Avenue, the shopping hub of the area, Midway contained 247,000 square feet of leasable space. Here the anchor grocery was a ShopRite. Pizza Hut, Dress Barn, Panera Bread, CVS, Jo-Ann Fabrics, Red Lobster and The People's United Bank were other tenants. With the closing on this property, the UBP portfolio had reached an even fifty properties with about 600 tenants.

On March 9, company chairman and CEO Charles J. Urstadt had pointed out to the Board of Directors that the relative lack of growth the previous year was at least partly a reflection of the competition presented by other REITs raising considerable sums through stock offerings and bidding up the price of properties that came on the market. It was a development that would eventually force a slight change in the Urstadt Biddle game plan, with a possible greater emphasis on limited ownerships and partnerships.

The June purchase of the Midway Shopping Center demonstrated UBP's flexibility and creativity in adapting its business plan to a still difficult acquisitions market, just as Mr. Urstadt had suggested it would do in March. The company became a general partner in the Midway center along with the families who had built and renovated it. Urstadt Biddle's 25 percent general partnership interest was good for a 10 percent equity interest. It also lent $11.6 million to the partnership to refinance already existing loans and would manage and lease the center. The bottom line is that for an outlay of only about $6 million, Urstadt Biddle, in an acquisition climate that was often stymieing other shopping center REITs, was able to add to its properties a significant neighborhood shopping center in its prime target area.

The year 2010 was another one in which the byword was "flat is the new 'good'." FFO was relatively steady, in fact down a bit on a per share basis. But that meant the ship was on course, moving straight ahead in waters a lot calmer than much of the competition experienced. The company managed to do some cost-cutting, but without having to lay off anyone from its already lean staff. Every possible revenue stream was being investigated, including leases from cell phone towers that were contributing to the bottom line. That theater in Carmel, New York was now being run by a new, rent-paying tenant and requests for rent reductions from company tenants had declined. If there was any doubt about how the public perceived the company's direction and the efficiency of its management, the 2.5 million shares of Class A Common Stock it sold in September at $18.05 per share, 92 percent of the highest value Urstadt Biddle's stock had reached over the previous year, represented a solid vote of confidence.

Definitely on the upside was the company's ability to be a good corporate citizen while making money for its shareholders. Among the innovative practices it put into effect in 2010 were an environmentally friendly parking lot at Airport Plaza in Danbury and construction of rooftop solar arrays on supermarkets at two other shopping centers. In the future they would lower not only energy costs for the stores but also carbon emissions to the tune of about 472 tons annually.

Another positive development in 2010 was the increased dividend on both classes of stock, up a penny per share. But on the downside, the recession was pushing school districts and municipalities to increase real estate taxes to make up for a shortfall from other revenues. That constituted a rising cost for existing REIT tenants and made it yet more challenging to sign new tenants.

As the worst of the recession faded with the end of the century's first decade, an important tie to Urstadt Biddle's origins also passed. Morry Hubbard, a Director Emeritus of Urstadt Biddle and a founder and guiding force behind HRE Properties, the company that would evolve into Urstadt Biddle Properties, died in September at age 101. Only three months later, the company also lost an active, seasoned Director with the passing of George J. Vojta. Mr. Vojta brought a strong banking and finance background to the Board and had served UBP for twelve years as a Director and a member of the Board's Audit and Nominating and Corporate Governance Committees.

New Challenges

Looking back at the past year in early 2011, Urstadt Biddle shared with its stockholders its sense of relief that the economic outlook had improved. "Well, we feel a lot better than we did a year ago!" the company's *2010 Annual Report* began. "The frightening scare is over. Credit markets have basically returned to normal. Retailers have cut costs, adapted to survive with a more cost-conscious consumer base and are looking to open stores again. The property markets have thawed and properties are trading again, albeit at aggressive cap rates."

The report might have added about the beginning of 2011 that at least the roof didn't fall in, although it could have. At UBP's shopping center in Meriden, Connecticut heavy snow caused the company to take the precaution of closing the center for five days while snow was removed from building roofs.

In some ways, 2011 was similar to the year that preceded it. Again the company added three major shopping centers to its portfolio, all in its target area. The first, in April, was the Fairfield Plaza Shopping Center in New Milford, Connecticut for just under $11 million, with the company assuming a $5 million mortgage maturing in 2015. As with the New Milford Plaza, which Urstadt Biddle purchased the previous year, Fairfield Plaza was located on busy Route 7 in the area north of Danbury. Anchored by Staples and T.J. Maxx, the shopping center's roster of tenants also included Sleepy's, Olympia Sports, Edible Arrangements, Sherwin Williams and Quiznos. Less than ten years old, the center added 72,000 square feet of leasable space to the company's inventory.

In October 2011 UBP tapped its unsecured line of credit to acquire the Fairfield Centre in Fairfield, Connecticut. For $17 million, Urstadt Biddle bought a mortgage-free, modest-sized center offering 63,300 square feet of leaseable space. All three stores on the property, located on Route 1, were leased to quality national retailers: CVS, Marshall's and Office Max. Willing Biddle noted at the time that the purchase fulfilled a company goal—"to acquire property in this densely populated and wealthy demographic area of Fairfield County."

The final acquisition of 2011, in December, was in Eastchester in Westchester County. Urstadt Biddle bought The Eastchester Plaza Shopping Center through a subsidiary for $9 million in cash and the assumption of a $3.6 million mortgage. More than half of the 23,300 square feet of space was anchored by a CVS drugstore, as was the center the company acquired in October. And this shopping center's location in lower Westchester County, on Route 22, was just as demographically advantageous as the center in Fairfield.

In 2011, Urstadt Biddle also continued its foray into the realm of cheaper and cleaner energy. Subsequent to completing the installation of solar panels at the company's Emerson and Wayne, New Jersey shopping centers, a similar array was being actively planned for the property in the Ironbound section of Newark and for other centers where government subsidies and financing available from utility companies made them a wise choice for less expensive power.

Financials offered a mixed picture for the year. FFO was flat, but mostly because of a technicality relating to the sale of Class A Common shares. Local real estate tax increases continued to be a drag on the company's bottom line, but revenues hit a new high of $91 million. Administrative expenses at about 1.3 percent of gross assets were excellent relative to the size of Urstadt Biddle and the company was taking advantage of historically low interest rates to mortgage one of its shopping centers to compensate for the use of its credit line to make acquisitions.

Leasing remained a concern, a lingering aftermath of the recession with its accompanying business caution and business failures. By mid-year floundering Blockbuster Video, as part of its nationwide bankruptcy restructuring, had rejected leases at three of its four Urstadt Biddle locations. While the amount of square footage throughout the portfolio that renewed at higher rents was twice the amount renewed at lower rents, the dollar value of the rent decreases offset the increases. Just as problematic was a decrease in total leased space to 90.5 percent, a drop of 3.1 percent from 2010. While renting that vacant space was of course a major goal, the company was cautious not to do it with long-term leases that locked in unnaturally low rents reflecting business conditions that, more likely than not, were going to improve.

But one part of the leasing picture was bright. In August about 55,000 square feet of space that had been vacated by a supermarket in the Townline Square Shopping Center in Meriden, Connecticut was leased to a Big Y World Class Market, a supermarket that already anchored two Urstadt Biddle centers. The company's joint investment with Big Y in renovating the space, costing a total of $3 million, would be well worth it, leading to an annual rental income of about $900,000.

To nobody's surprise, Urstadt Biddle in 2011 not only continued its uninterrupted dividend payments—forty-two years and counting—but, as in 2010, increased them by a penny a share for both Common and Class A Common Stock. This represented the 18th consecutive annual increase in the company's dividends on its common stock. While the price of the UBP shares, which had weathered the recession very nicely, reflected the continuity of this healthy tradition, it wasn't the only index of the company's financial quality registered in 2011. In March, the financial services firm of Keefe, Bruyette & Woods introduced its first REIT Dividend Honor Roll. The "Honor Roll represents REITS that have had a solid track record of increasing/maintaining their dividend from 2000 to 2010, including the financial crisis when many REITs substantially cut their dividend in an effort to preserve capital," they explained. The list honored only fourteen REITs of all kinds and sizes. Urstadt Biddle, with the smallest market capitalization of any firm on the list, came in tenth.

After twenty-one years, Peter Herrick resigned from Urstadt Biddle's Board of Directors in 2011. Chairman and CEO Charles J. Urstadt, after expressing his appreciation of Mr. Herrick's services, said of his replacement, Richard Grellier, who had previously served as a consultant to the company, that "he brings with him over 25 years of real estate experience, including 17 years as a real estate investment banker, special knowledge of the retail REIT sector and experience in capital markets solutions."

UBP's first acquisition in 2012 was a DownReit transaction in which Urstadt Biddle became the sole managing partner in a new limited liability company. It also represented an initial venture into a new part of the company's target area for acquisitions. The Orangetown Shopping Center, with 75,000 square feet of leasable space, anchored by a CVS drugstore, included among its diversified tenants Dunkin Donuts, a Subway sandwich shop, Allstate insurance office, an Orange Farm Market, Planet Wings, Twins India Palace and the Palisades Federal Savings Bank. It was 96 percent occupied and just as importantly, as Willing Biddle stated, "We are excited to have added our first shopping center in Rockland County, New York. This investment will be the platform for UBP to expand its footprint in Rockland County, one of the few high demographic counties surrounding New York City in which the company had not previously been invested."

By the beginning of 2012, it may not exactly have been "morning in America," but at least the sun was out again and most businesses, including REITs, were seeing something close to a normal business climate. In fact, many people were seeing REITs as one of the better investments available. On March 5, *Barron's*, in a roundtable discussion on real estate, summarized its analysts' outlook: "The housing market may be flat on its back, but real estate investment trusts are doing just fine, thank you." Three days later Baird Equity Research featured one shopping center REIT that was doing especially well: Urstadt Biddle Properties. "We remain buyers of the shares at current levels," Baird stated, "and view the shares as particularly attractive for income-oriented investors." A month later, the investment website *Seeking Alpha* proposed UBP as a prime example of a REIT whose "steady growth" based on a proven business plan was a company worth looking into.

And yet for shopping center REITs, including UBP, there were new challenges and some clouds on the horizon. Held over from the recession was a tough climate in which to increase rents. Similarly, vacancies were taking longer to fill. Credit was still tight and it took a strong stomach for anyone to initiate a sole proprietorship and sign a lease that would satisfy both tenant and shopping center owner.

Some longer-range challenges had been looming on the horizon for awhile. For example, catalog sales of everything from gifts to shoes, always competition for brick and mortar stores, were increasing. Direct delivery of meals from services such as Fresh Direct competed with supermarket sales, particularly in upscale areas. And looming over many of the kinds of businesses that were likely to provide tenants for Urstadt Biddle shopping centers was the Internet. One or two clicks of a mouse and a plethora of products could be on their way to your front door without your foot ever touching a gas pedal. Internet giants such as Amazon not only were putting bookstores out of business—Border's had been an Urstadt Biddle tenant—they were selling food and clothing as well. The ubiquitous smart phone with its access to everything on the Internet was becoming an essential shopping tool; swiped over a bar code to compare prices, it often sent its user to the competition or to the computer to order online, not only paying a lower price reflecting the Internet merchandiser's virtual lack of overhead, but also possibly avoiding the sales tax they would have paid in a store.

Over the years UBP had dealt with many changes in the real estate market and in consumer shopping habits, and it would make the necessary adjustments to current trends as well. Senior management had under consideration various new ways to grow the business, including possible websites for its neighborhood shopping centers—alerting consumers to sales and "specials," allowing customers to determine if a particular product was in stock and reserving it for pick-up—possible direct operation of franchises by UBP and much more.

The company was also developing new ways to maximize returns on its assets. Cell phone tower rental space and energy savings through participation in solar energy programs were only two of those ways. Increased use of shopping center space for advertising was under consideration, and also on the table were some tentative plans to use shopping center space for retail operations that would directly involve Urstadt Biddle. One very valuable asset already producing a revenue stream for UBP was the cumulative experience and know-how of its thirty-six employees. That asset was employed in managing shopping centers owned by other companies as well as its own, a valuable contribution to UBP's revenue stream.

After "The Great Recession," financial soothsayers were a lot more hesitant to predict the future than they had been. But it was a reasonably good bet that a company that had now paid uninterrupted dividends for forty-three years, including right through the recent financial crisis, which also had the highest inside ownership of any REIT and thus was run by management with a personal interest in UBP's prosperity, would successfully handle any challenge the future would bring.

Appendix I

Urstadt Biddle Properties' goals and the way the company is organized and functions to secure its objectives have been set forth by CEO Charles J. Urstadt:

MISSION STATEMENT

Urstadt Biddle Properties is a simple business compared to more complex corporate undertakings. We are a self-administered real estate investment trust that aims to seek out and buy properties, predominantly supermarket-anchored shopping centers, in one of the most affluent areas of the United States. By carefully selecting these properties, paying for them in ways most advantageous to our business, upgrading and maintaining the properties and leasing space in them to the best possible tenants at the best possible terms, all the while keeping our operation as efficient as possible, we make a profit. That profit has resulted in 38 consecutive years of uninterrupted dividends for our stockholders. We have done this in the past, and will continue to do so in the future by keeping in mind that our approach must be dynamic and not immutable. We have to be flexible, always keeping our eyes on the success of our "bottom line."

ORGANIZING TO CARRY OUT THE MISSION

Like all organizations our personnel are organized into STAFF and LINE.

I. STAFF

The Staff, which supports the front line, is headed by the Chief Executive Officer ("CEO") and the Chief Operating Officer ("COO") who interface with the Board of Directors. The Board, in turn, is responsible to the Shareholders who own the Company. Reporting to the CEO and COO are:

(a) Finance

Responsible for accounting and finance but also handles insurance and office management.

(b) Legal

Covers Corporate regulatory matters, governance issues and Real Estate acquisitions and leasing.

II. LINE

The Line organizations also reporting to the CEO and COO are:

(a) Acquisitions
(b) Leasing
(c) Management

THE PIPELINE: HOW IT ALL WORKS IN PRACTICE

I. **Acquire**

The Acquisitions Department must be energetic and aggressive in seeking out properties that meet our standards.

At the present time our target area is Westchester, Fairfield, Putnam, Northern New Jersey and Long Island. Our target properties are grocery-anchored shopping centers, but we must also consider close by office buildings, where we also have experience. We are not the largest bidder for these properties, so we must rely on our strengths.

First of all we are a public company that can offer a "DownReit" opportunity. That gives us an advantage over private buyers, especially where there is a difference of opinion between multiple owners of the selling properties, some of which want cash and some of which want Opportunity Partnership Units. Our approach is to accumulate as much information on target properties as possible and get well acquainted with their owners, which means constant contact so when they decide to sell they have us in mind.

Our second strength is "patience". It usually takes a long time for sellers to make up their minds. If they know us and our reputation and we stay in contact with them we will succeed. We have many examples where our patience has paid off.

II. Finance

The second step in the pipeline is to pay for the properties we acquire. We have many sources of finance. These include (a) banks—short term loans and mortgages; (b) investment banks—common and preferred stock and bonds; and (c) sales of non-core properties.

The Finance Department must anticipate cash needs and find the appropriate methods which are most beneficial to the company. This involves complex computation and comparison of maturity and interest rates.

III. Leasing

We want the best tenants paying the best rents with the highest occupancy rate. It is not easy. We always aim to sell the immediate rent to the tenant with an eye toward the future and not give away too much on renewals, options or tenant improvement expenses. It is an axiom that 100% occupancy means the rents are too low. Corporate management should not second guess the leasing agents who are in the front lines.

We always keep in mind the ever present threat of inflation and try to protect us against it. How? Short leases, no options, generous escalation for taxes and Common Area Maintenance.

IV. Management

Management has two goals—the first is to maintain the properties so that they are attractive to our tenants and their customers. That means shopping for the best prices from vendors and constant supervision of each property for problems and necessary corrections.

The second is to collect the rent, which is a shared task between management and the accounting department. Most important is to keep the arrears down and stay after tenants because experience shows that the further back a tenant gets in the rent the more likely he is to default.

And finally

V. Pay Dividends

After the first four steps are done there must be a profit (Funds from Operations) to cover the dividend and whenever prudent, increase it, because without the stockholders and their investment in this company, we would all be out of work.

UBP'S CONSTITUENCIES

Essentially, we work for the following constituencies. We have legal obligation to lenders, to our preferred stockholders, to our tenants and to our payees and government, while our obligation to our common stockholders, employees and customers of the centers is moral.

I. INVESTORS

    (a) Shareholders—Common and Preferred. We are legally bound to pay the Preferred shareholders the agreed dividend rate. To Class A and Common shareholders we have a duty to pay a dividend dependent upon our profits and outlook. We also should have an obligation to maintain or increase the dividend whenever prudent.

II. EMPLOYEES—we are obligated to pay fair salaries and benefits so as to obtain and keep the highest quality personnel.

III. TENANTS—they pay the rent (approximately 80 million dollars a year) to make all this possible and should be treated with the utmost consideration and be provided with excellent facilities, but we should also realize that we must get at least market rents.

IV. CUSTOMERS—are the people who visit our centers (which we estimate to be about 20 million a year) who provide the income to our Tenants which eventually results in rents. Again, they deserve to be treated with the utmost consideration and be provided with excellent facilities.

V. PAYEES

    (a) For services such as accountants, lawyers, architects, brokers etc.
    (b) For goods, such as contractors and utilities

VI. GOVERNMENT—Federal, State, Local Governments, to which we pay taxes and other fees;

VII. ENVIRONMENT—self-evident

Appendix II

BASIC PRINCIPLES

In 1989 the company set forth the five basic principles by which its business would be guided:

1) Stick to one type of property: retail
2) Directly manage those properties
3) Only buy property within a limited area: Westchester and Putnam Counties in New York and Fairfield County in Connecticut; and Northern New Jersey and Long Island
4) Keep debt (mortgages and preferred stock) relatively low
5) Avoid partnerships wherever possible

Index

A

A&P, 74
Acquisitions Department, 144
acquisitions, characteristics of, 72
advisor, 12, 14, 19, 22, 24, 25, 26, 28, 29, 30, 33, 35, 36, 37, 38, 39, 43, 46, 47, 50, 51, 52, 53
   disposing of the, 49
   relationship with board of trustees, 24
   role of, 9
   services of, 26
advisory agreement
   Hubbard Real Estate Investment and Merrill Lynch Hubbard, 54
advisory body. *See* advisor; Merrill Lynch; Hubbard, Westervelt
Airport Plaza Shopping Center, 110
Alpha Beta Acme Markets, 24
annual reports, 27, 30, 33, 37, 39, 41, 42, 43, 44, 45, 46, 47, 53, 55, 57, 60, 61, 65, 66, 67, 68, 70, 71, 73, 75, 78, 79, 81, 86, 90, 93, 97, 98, 100, 103, 104, 110, 117, 120, 122
apartment buildings, 39, 44, 94, 113
Arcadian Shopping Center, 94, 99, 120
Argila, Raymond P., 68, 102
Aries, James, 110, 119
Arthur Andersen LLP, 20
Ashland Oil, 24

Asset Management Group, 77
Audit Committee, 27, 68

B

bank buildings, 39
bankruptcies, 35, 70, 73, 76, 85, 86, 88, 91, 92, 95, 96, 100, 105, 123
bankruptcy laws, 34
Bed Bath & Beyond, 78, 91, 99, 110, 121
Bessemer Securities Corporation, 22
Best of Industry Annual Report Awards, 41
Bi-County Shopping Center, 76, 118
Biddle, Willing Wing, 77, 81, 88, 89, 90, 92, 94, 97, 99, 101, 102, 105, 106, 111, 115, 116, 117, 119, 120, 121, 124, 125
   article in *Real Estate Weekly*, 99
Big Party!, 92
big-box stores, 91, 111, 123
Biltmore Shopping Center, 119
Block, Ralph L.
   Investing in REITs
   Real Estate Investment Trusts, 11
Blockbuster Video, 118
board of director's meetings, 90, 100, 102, 120, 122
   minutes of, 106
board of directors, 9, 44, 54, 96, 117, 143

board of governors, 28
board of trustees, 9, 17, 19, 20, 22, 24, 26, 27, 33, 36, 37, 39, 41, 46, 53, 54, 56, 57, 59, 60, 62, 68, 71, 73, 80, 86, 89
  change to board of directors, 90
  relationship with advisor, 24
board of trustees' meetings, 20, 35, 38, 39, 42, 56, 90
  minutes of, 17, 20, 25, 26, 30, 39, 41, 49, 50, 51, 52, 55, 56, 57, 58, 60, 67, 71, 86, 87, 97
Borders Books and Records, 113
Bradlees, 76, 85, 88, 91, 124
Bradley Real Estate Investors, 10
Briarcliff Manor, New York, 104
Broadway-Hale department store, 24
Burlington Coat Factory, 105
Burnham Pacific Properties, 14
business strategy, description of, 79

C

Caldor, 36, 88, 91, 96
  bankrupty of, 85
capital gains, 12, 81, 94
Carmel, New York, 81
cash flow, 10, 27, 28, 33, 42, 46, 60, 66, 67, 70, 71, 76, 80, 87, 114, 123
cash flow management, 28
Changing Times, 67
Channel Home Centers, 49, 70
Chase Manhattan Bank, 71, 77
Chateau Properties, 15
Chilmark Shopping Center, 104
Christmas Tree Shops, 99
Chrysler, 23, 24, 25, 40, 42, 70, 81, 96
Cigar Excise Tax Extension, 7
City Center, 113
Civic Center Plaza Towers, 49

Clearwater property, 87
Cleary, Martin, 38, 55, 57
Clifton, New Jersey, 99
closed-end REITs, 10
Coburn, Ralph G., 19, 20, 25, 27, 28, 30, 33, 34, 37, 38
commercial properties, 49
common shares, 55, 85, 89, 93, 125
  Class A, 103, 117
common stock, 10, 13, 17, 90, 100, 103, 124, 145
  Class A, 93, 101, 103, 114, 116, 123, 124
Compensation Committee, 57
conflict of interest, 19
Conklin, George T., Jr., 20, 59, 75
Connecticut, 72, 78, 94
Connecticut General Life Insurance Company (CIGNA), 38
Continental Mortgage Investors, 10, 11
Conway, E. Virgil, 57, 59
Cooper, Milton, 56, 57, 87
core business, 71, 124
corporate credit rating, 93
corporate governance, 106
cost control, 71
Countryside Village Shopping Center, 49, 105

D

Daffy's, 121
Danbury Square Shopping Center, 78, 88, 100
Danbury, Connecticut, 110
Darien, Connecticut, 119
Davis, Charles, 119
Dayton Hudson, 40
Decker, Mark, 101, 102
Decker, Mark, Jr., 101

Delafield Asset Management, 60
Denver, 46, 105
Denver property, 47, 77
depreciation, 27
DeWitt, New York, 49
diversification, 44, 47
dividend reinvestment plan, 46
dividends, 9, 22, 26, 27, 29, 33, 49, 67, 75,
　　86, 93, 100, 103, 143, 145
dividends, REITs, 13
Dock, 118, 123, 124
Douglass, Robert R., 71
Dow Jones Average, 103
DownREIT, 91, 144
DownREIT partnership, 94

E

E. A. Pierce, 17
Eastchester Mall, 91
Ecker, Howard L., 48
e-commerce, 97
Economic Recovery Act, 1981, 12
Educational Warehouse, 113
Eisenhower, Dwight, 8
Emerson, New Jersey, 124
Emerson Plaza, 124
Empire State Development Corporation, 37
entrepreneurship, 7, 18
Equity Group Investments, 11
equity investments, 29
Equity Lifestyle Properties, 11
equity market capitalization, 14
Equity Office Properties Trust, 11, 15
equity REITs, 9, 10, 11, 12, 14, 16
Equity Residential, 11, 15
Ernst & Young, 123
Executive Committee, 27, 38
Executive Compensation and Stock
　　Option Committee, 53

F

Fairfield County Business Journal, 115
Fairfield County, Connecticut, 94, 110, 121, 147
Farmingdale, Long Island (New York), 75, 118
Federal, 86
federal tax code, 53
Ferris, Baker Watts (FBW), 101
Finance Department, 145
Financial Planning, 13, 103
Financial World, 41
First Boston Corporation, 58
First Mortgage Fund, 10
First Mortgage Investors, 10
First Union Real Estate, 10
First Union Realty Trust, 51
Fitch Duff & Phelps, 100
Five Town Plaza, 86, 92, 96, 116
Food Emporium, 92
Forbes, 10, 35
　REIT rating list, 15
401(k) plans, 15
funds from operations (FFO), 13, 15, 65, 67, 68, 71, 75, 77, 80, 85, 86, 87, 93, 97, 100, 103, 104, 114, 117, 119, 123, 145

G

Galleria Shopping Center, 113
Gap, 99
Garday, Louis J., 14
Giffels Associates, 47, 70, 105
Giffels Office Building, 46, 48, 88, 120
go-gets, 64
golden parachutes, 57, 58
Goldman Sachs, 52, 58, 59
Goldstein, Sanford, 36
Goodwives Shopping Center, 94, 105, 122

Grand Union, 95
  bankruptcy of, 105
Green Farms Plaza Shopping Center, 115
Green Street Advisors, 86
Greenwich, Connecticut, 75, 78, 80, 91, 103, 104
Gristede's Shopping Center, 122
Gristede's Supermarket, 95
gross income, 9, 26

H

Hagen, Stephen C., 38, 39, 42, 54, 59, 75
Hall, Brinley M., 27, 54
health clubs, 111
Hecht's, 36, 69, 81
Heritage 202 Center, 72, 73, 88, 95
Heritage Hills Development Corporation, 72, 73
Heritage Hills Shopping Center, 73
Herman's, 88
Herrick, Peter, 68
Hess, Dennis, 51
Hilliard Lyons, 102
Houston, 46, 48, 67, 81, 87
Houston property, 39, 80
HRE Properties, Inc., 60, 76, 77, 90, *See also* UBP
  acquisitions, 74, 75, 76, 78, 79, 80, 81, 87, 88, 92, 93
  annual reports, 60, 61, 65, 66, 67, 68, 70, 71, 73, 75, 78, 79, 81, 86
  board meetings, 90
    minutes of, 60, 67, 71, 86, 87
  board of trustees, 60, 62, 68, 71, 73, 80, 86, 89
  portfolio, 67
  renaming to UBP, 90
  reorganization, 90
HREI (Hubbard Real Estate Investments), 12, 16, 17, 19, 20, 27, 35, 37, 40, 44, 48, 50, 75, 77, 90, *See also* UBP
  acquisitions, 24, 26, 28, 30, 46, 49, 66, 72
  annual reports, 27, 30, 33, 37, 39, 41, 42, 43, 44, 45, 46, 47, 53, 55, 57, 65
  board meetings, 20, 35, 38, 39, 56
    minutes of, 17, 20, 25, 26, 30, 39, 41, 49, 50, 51, 52, 55, 56, 57, 58
  board of trustees, 9, 17, 20, 22, 24, 26, 27, 33, 36, 37, 39, 41, 46, 53, 54, 56, 57, 59
  history of, 19
  investment program, 27
  membership in NAREIT, 27
  portfolio, 42, 43, 48, 53, 55
  portfolio, meeting, 22
  relocation to Boston, 20
Hubanita, 77
Hubbard Advisory Corporation, 50, 80
Hubbard Property Management, 36
Hubbard, George Morry, Jr., 19, 30, 36, 38, 54, 77
Hubbard, John C., 19, 27, 30, 34, 54, 77
Hubbard, Westervelt & Mottelay, 19, 24, 25, 26, 38

I

IBM, 73
Imhof, Linda, 99
industrial properties, 22, 70, 91
inflation, 7, 29, 33, 43, 67, 79, 145
  in the 1970s, 11
Internal Revenue Code of 1954, 7
International Harvester, 28
International Herald Tribune, 16

Internet shopping, 97
Investing in REITs Real Estate Investment Trusts (Block), 11
Investment Dealer's Digest, 15, 16
investment portfolio, 9, 33
iParty Corporation, 92
IPOs (initial public offerings), 13, 16, 17, 20, 46

J

J. Henry Schroder Banking Corporation, 34
Jamesway, 85, 91
  bankruptcy of, 86
joint ventures, 44, 46, 77, 105
Journal of Financial Planning, 16

K

Kent, John, 74, 75
Kimco Development Corporation. *See* Kimco Realty Corporation
Kimco Realty Corporation, 15, 55, 56, 57, 58, 59, 60, 67, 69, 86, 87, 105
  acquisitions, 117
  attempt to take over HRE, 55, 60
  going public, 13
Kimmel, Martin, 56
King Kullen Supermarket, 76
Kmart, 35, 36, 40, 41, 70, 113
Knight Ridder, 98

L

LA Fitness Sports Clubs, 111
Lacey, Linda, 119
Landauer, James, 51
Larsen, Leslie, 80
Lawrence, George H. C., 57, 60

Leasing Department, 145
LeFrak, Sam, 28
Lenz, Winthrop, 17, 19
Levites Realty Management Corp., 77
limited partnerships, 8, 12, 44
Linens 'n Things, 76, 99, 105
Long Island, New York, 76
Los Angeles property, 75
Lurie, Robert, 11

M

Magowan, Robert A., 23
Management, 145
Manassas, Virginia, 36, 69, 81
Marlborough, Massachusetts, 47
Marshals, 110
Massachusetts, 20, 30
Massachusetts Investor's Trust, 8
Mawhinney, Joyce, 75
McDonald's, 113
Meck, John F., 20
medical office building, 104
Melville Corp., 110
Meriden, Connecticut, 75
Merrill Lynch, 8, 17, 18, 19, 22, 24, 34, 42, 51, 52, 57, 58, 80
Merrill Lynch Capital Markets, 58
Merrill Lynch Hubbard, 38, 50, 51, 52, 53, 55, *See also* Merrill Lynch
Merrill Lynch Realty, Inc., 51
Merrill, Charles, 17, 23
Merrill, Lynch, Pierce, Fenner & Smith. *See* Merrill Lynch
Merritt, John C., 88, 94, 113
Michaels Crafts, 110
Mid-Atlantic Realty Trust, 117
Mitchell-Lama (law), 29
mixed-use facility, 54, 74, 78, 92
money-saving measure, 27

Mooney, James L., 38
Moore, James Jim R., 54, 59, 60, 91, 100, 102, 112
Moorestown, New Jersey, 121
Morgan Keegan, 102
mortgage REITs, 11, 29
Motley Fool, 120
Mueller, Robert J., 117
Multifoods, 80
Murdoch, Molly (William F. Murdoch's daughter), 41
Murdoch, William F., Jr., 25, 34, 35, 38, 40, 41, 47, 48, 51, 53, 57, 58, 59, 71
mutual fund industry, 8
mutual funds, stock, 12, 44
Myers, Thomas D., 77, 92

N

NAREIT All REIT index, 93, 114
NAREIT Equity index, 103
NAREIT index, 11, 28, 95
National Association of Real Estate Investment Trusts (NAREIT), 11, 15, 16, 28, 103, 110
 forum, 106
National Real Estate Investor, 14, 106
National Real Estate Stock Fund, 13
net income, 27, 67
New Plan Realty Trust, 14, 86
New York, 13, 28, 38, 50, 72, 101
New York Construction News, 90
New York Stock Exchange, 11, 16, 20, 26, 54, 59, 106, 117
New York Times, 13, 59, 72, 73, 113, 116, 121
Newington property, 74
NIMBY (not in my backyard), 72
9/11, 101, 102, 103
noncore assets, 80, 87, 88, 95, 96, 98, 101, 105, 120

O

office buildings, 11, 37, 39, 40, 44, 45, 46, 47, 48, 49, 67, 70, 71, 74, 75, 76, 78, 80, 81, 87, 91, 94, 95, 104, 105, 110, 114, 116, 119, 120, 124, 125, 144
OfficeMax, 113, 121
Old Navy, 76, 99, 105, 110
One Denver Highlands, 46, 88
operating costs, 71
Opportunity Partnership Units, 144
Orange Meadows Shopping Center, 112, 115
Orange, Connecticut, 112
Ossining, New York, 119
Outback Steakhouse, 113
overbuilding, 11, 12, 67, 68, 77
overbuilding, role of REITs in, 11

P

Paganucci, Paul D., 54, 55, 60
passive investment, 12
Pearce, Urstadt, Mayer & Greer, Inc., 38, 56, 91
Pennsylvania REIT, 10
pension plans, 15
Pepsico, 73
Peregrine, Inc., 88
Petco, 118
Phillips International, Inc., 74
Pier One Imports, 115
plant closings, 42
portfolio, 14, 39, 53
portfolio, creating, 22
portfolio, REIT's, 9
preferred stock, 117, 145
 offering, 30, 93

rating, 100, 125
sale of, 93, 125
　Series C, 115
　Series D, 120
　UBP's Series B, 105
Project Review Committee, 52
Property Management Manual, 81
Property Sales Committee, 80
Putnam County, New York, 147

R

RadioShack, 104, 115
real estate industry, 7, 11, 12, 39, 44, 66, 67, 68
Real Estate Investment Trust Act, 7, 9
real estate investments, types of, 11
Real Estate Research Corporation, 25
Real Estate Weekly, 94, 99, 104
Realty Stock Review, 11
recession, 11, 14, 40, 68, 70
　1982, 47
Regan, Donald, 52
REIT Capital Trust, Inc., 11
REIT Improvement Act, 2004, 15
REITs (real estate investment trusts), 7, 9, 12, 13, 14, 16, 20, 29, 33, 53, 56, 65, 90, 98, 103, 143
　benefits on sale leasebacks, 18
　close-end, 10
　dividends, 13, 22
　emergence of, 10, 11
　equity, 9, 10, 11, 12, 14, 16
　going public, 16
　gross income, 9, 26
　growth of, 16, 22
　in S&P 500 index, 15
　law, 10, 25
　mortgage, 11, 29
　rating list by *Forbes*, 15
　residential, 15

role in overbuilding, 11
　share price, 15
rent increases, 36, 39
residential REIT, 15
Ridgefield Center, 92, 96
Ridgefield, Connecticut, 88, 94
Ridgeway Shopping Center, 110, 111, 114, 120, 123
Rockefeller, Nelson A., 38, 71
Rockefeller Center Properties, 13
Roslyn, Long Island (New York), 13, 60
Rye, New York, 119

S

S&P 500 index, 14, 16, *See also* Standard & Poor's
Safeway Stores, 23, 25, 40, 48, 69
sale leasebacks, 17, 18, 19, 22, 23, 24, 29, 39, 43, 44
Salm, Harold, 54
Santa Anita Realty Enterprises, Inc., 49, 77
Saratoga, New York, 26
Sarbanes-Oxley Act, 15, 105, 110, 120, 123
Schroder Real Estate Corporation, 34
Securities and Exchange Commission (SEC), 15, 106
　Schedule 13D, 60
　Schedule 14D, 56
self-management, 53
Senior Planning Committee, 117
Series A Participating Preferred Shares, 57
share prices, 15, 35, 59, 60, 68, 86, 87
share value, 13
shareholder rights plan, 57
Shaw's Supermarkets, 118, 119, 122
Shoppes at Eastchester, 120
Shopping Center World, 91

shopping centers, 14, 33, 44, 49, 54, 55, 56, 62, 63, 69, 70, 71, 72, 74, 75, 76, 78, 79, 81, 85, 86, 87, 88, 91, 92, 94, 95, 97, 99, 100, 101, 103, 104, 105, 110, 111, 112, 113, 115, 116, 117, 118, 119, 120, 122, 124, 143, 144
shopping malls. *See* shopping centers
ShopRite, 76, 81, 88, 92, 96, 124
Shufro, Rose & Ehrman, 60
Silverstein, Larry, 110
Simon Property Group, 15
Small Business Magazine, 114
Sneaker Stadium, 88
Somers Shopping Center, 73
Somers, New York, 72, 73, 95, 115
Southern Plaza, 87
Southfield, Michigan, 46, 48, 70, 80, 88, 105, 116, 119, 120
Spag: An American Business Legend (Borgatti), 96
Spag's Supply, Inc., 96
Spangler, Richard, 51
Sports Authority, 113
Springfield Shopping Center, 54
Springfield, Massachusetts, 49, 69, 70, 78, 85, 86, 96
Stamford, Connecticut, 110, 124
Standard & Poor's, 16, 103
Standard & Poor's REIT Composite index, 117, *See also* Standard & Poor's
Staples, 110, 118
Staples Plaza, 120
Starbucks, 116
Starbucks Plaza, 124
step-down rents, 18, 40, 42, 43, 49
stock market, 8, 14
  1987 crash of, 13, 67
stockbrokers, 10, 102
Stop & Shop Supermarket, 88, 94, 110, 115, 119

Stratford, Connecticut, 118
Super Stop & Shop, 118
supermarket chains, 23, 24, 40, 69, 74, 81, 91, 92, 95, 97, 101, 123

T

Taggart, Joseph, 20
Taubman Centers, 15
  going public, 14
Taubman, A. Alfred, 14
Tax Reform Act, 1976, 12
Tax Reform Act, 1986, 12
tax shelters, 12
tenants, 18, 23, 33, 35, 39, 42, 46, 47, 49, 70, 73, 76, 78, 80, 81, 85, 86, 88, 94, 95, 96, 99, 100, 101, 104, 105, 110, 111, 113, 115, 118, 121, 123, 124
terrorism insurance, 102
Towne Centre, 95, 96
Townline Square Shopping Center, 75, 91, 99, 105, 114
ToysRUs, 78, 113
Trader Joe's, 112
Two-Buck Chuck (wine), 112

U

UBP (Urstadt Biddle Properties, Inc.), 7, 9, 12, 15, 16, 17, 57, 59, 66, 89, 90, 95, 104, 105, 106, 114, 115, 116, 124
  acquisitions, 55, 94, 95, 104, 110, 112, 114, 115, 118, 119, 120, 121, 122, 124
  annual reports, 90, 93, 97, 98, 100, 103, 104, 110, 117, 120, 122
  basic principles, 147
  board meetings
    minutes of, 97

board of directors, 96, 117, 143
constituencies, 146
credit corporate rating, 1998, 93
growth of, 91
mission statement, 143
personnel, 143
portfolio, 72, 93, 96, 98, 104, 119, 122, 123, 124, 125
stock sale, 94
Unitco Realty and Construction Co., Inc., 18
Urstadt, Charles D., 89
Urstadt, Charles J., 13, 29, 30, 38, 47, 52, 55, 56, 59, 60, 63, 64, 73, 86, 88, 89, 93, 97, 100, 101, 102, 111, 114, 116, 117, 122, 125
  articles in *Real Estate Weekly*, 94, 104
  business philosophy, 62
  election as CEO, 62
  membership in board of trustees, 37
  operational philosophy, 64
  professional and educational background, 38
  To Our Shareholders message, 65, 66, 70

V

Valley Ridge Shopping Center, 74
Valley, Matt, 106
Value City Department Stores, Inc., 92
Vojta, George J., 96
Vornado, 22, 86

W

W. T. Grant Company, 17, 23, 24, 33, 34, 37, 41
  bankruptcy of, 35, 43
Wall Street Journal, 11, 14, 54, 56, 70, 80
Washington Mutual, 116
Washington REIT, 10
Wayne, New Jersey, 74, 101
Weingarten, 86
Wertheim Schroder & Company, 59
Westchester Community College, 99
Westchester County Business Journal, 101, 112
Westchester County, New York, 71, 94, 110, 121, 124, 147
Westchester Pavilion Shopping Center, 112, 113, 116, 121
Westport, Connecticut, 115
WFC Holdings Corporation, 125
Whitehead, John, 52
White Plains, New York, 91
Willis, Richard S., 20, 37
Willow Lake Village, 29
Wirth, Wayne, 92
Wiz, 76, 88, 91, 105
  bankruptcy of, 76

Y

York, James O., 41, 60, 96
Young, Bryant, 54, 74

Z

Zeckendorf, William, 38
Zell, Sam, 11, 15

Edwards Brothers Malloy
Thorofare, NJ USA
September 16, 2013